After being educated in America, Belgium, France, England and Wales, Jodi Hyland joined the *Southport Visiter and Journal* where, after only three weeks, she was given her own page. She spent the war years in intelligence at Bletchley Park, then joined *Woman's Own* as a feature writer and later features editor. She spent two years in Sydney and returned to edit a number of women's magazines, culminating with *Woman's Mirror*, where she married the boss and became Jodi Cudlipp.

THE SAWDUST MILLIONAIRE

Jodi Cudlipp

Revel Barker
Publishing

First published by Revel Barker Publishing, 2010
Copyright © Jodi Lady Cudlipp 2010

ISBN: 978-0-9563686-4-5

Revel Barker Publishing
66 Florence Road
Brighton BN2 8DJ
England

revelbarker@gmail.com

DEDICATION
To Johnny, Marion and Mark,
the helpful crew on this voyage

Foreword

When my husband and I first met Johnny Inkster, he had his boat next to ours in a southern county marina. We didn't know much about him, except somebody told us he was a sawdust merchant, but we didn't know what that meant. We didn't even then know his name – so, because his boat was bigger than ours and because he and his family (wife and two small children) arrived in a smart car, we called him the Sawdust Millionaire.

Of course we had no idea of the depth or otherwise of his bank account, but in our eyes he acted like a millionaire – and had we been in the casting business, we would have cast him as such. Here's a 'for instance': when the chandlery at the marina was not doing so well and was up for sale Johnny bought the entire contents – ropes, engines, anchors, yachting shoes and clothing, sea-scooters and all. He put a sale price on each item, and when all was sold up he had made a neat profit.

When we got to know him better it was clear that – whether a millionaire or not, here was a man who could turn an honest penny in more than one way – he was a hard worker with a good head and to my mind an example not only to his own children, but to the youth of today… the youth of today, who love money to spend and often think, or dream, that it can come some easy way via crime or lottery, or by aping a football hero or pop singer.

Johnny achieved his dream, always counted in pence, pounds and maximum thousands, never millions, by hard work and guile – and the story of his life shows that it can be done. Millionaire? – I have no idea and don't care; what is important is how he turned those honest pence into a small – sometimes large – profit by using his bright brain, quick talk and industry.

He is now of an age where many men retire, but Johnny works on, enjoying what he does to achieve the next sweet dream.

Chapter One
In the beginning...

Johnny Inkster is a one off. You might never meet another like him. But how to describe him, to define his charm...? Handsome? Yes. Amusing? Yes. Good company? Oh yes. Caring? Yes – particularly of his own family. Good talker? Oh, my God, Yes, with a capital Y. He's a born raconteur. One story after another gallops along, all told with colourful detail, in his typical East London way, dotted here and there with a Cockney phrase.

His 'Holy Grail' when he left school at sixteen was to be a farmer, and then to be a millionaire. It was also the ambition of a police sergeant father for his son. Not, of course, via crime, but it was difficult to know at that time in that place how else it could be achieved. It was just over halfway through the twentieth century, at Hainault, an East London suburb at the end of the underground Central line.

Britain in the fifties was a dull place for a young man. The country was still throwing off the shackles held over from the war and rationing. The most cheering event was the coronation of the young Queen in 1953, dampened by the ceaseless rain of that day, but warmed by the sunny smile of the enormous Queen of Tonga, impervious to the downpour in her open carriage.

The occasion itself sold television sets to thousands of Britons who until then had remained loyal to the BBC radio that had been their friend, informant, educator and entertainer through the blacked-out dark days of the war. How were they going to give up the rich but neutral tones of Stewart Hibbard and Alvar Lidell for the pretty boys of TV? How would the ironing be done on a Saturday without *Saturday Night Theatre*? What would you laugh at without Tommy Handley's *TTFN* or the happy lunacy of Spike Milligan's Eccles squeaking such memorable inanities as 'Needle Nardle Noo!, to name but a few', or 'Ying tong iddle I po'? Or would we desert the nardle-noo to name records of Frank Sinatra or Elvis Presley or hold our breaths for the next instalment of *Quatermass*? Well, we did in the end, but not until we had bought our own TV sets for the coronation, or become addicted after watching on a neighbour's set.

To some people – Johnny's mother, for example – World War Two had been the most interesting, vivid and exciting thing that had ever happened and nothing would ever be like that again. They were the best years of her life.

The blacked-out semi-detached house where the family lived from 1938 overlooked a sports field and farmland. It was one mile, as the aircrews flew, to RAF Fairlop aerodrome from which Spitfires and Hurricanes defended London from the German bombers. Twelve miles away was London's East End, with good views of the Luftwaffe planes arriving and the fires of London they lit, so there was plenty for Winifred (Win to her friends) to talk about while remaining about ninety percent safe from German harm. As the family had their own chickens scratching in the back garden, the egg ration was unimportant and there was an occasional bird for Sunday lunch. She enjoyed the gossip with friends and strangers while queuing at local shops for any extras.

Win was not alone in her enjoyment of wartime, although not many perhaps would have admitted it. But by

9

the time a pre-war housewife had aged beyond the days of courtship and childbearing, life just seemed to have become a boring drudgery of keeping the home clean and tidy, coping with a family and cooking an evening meal for the returning breadwinner. To the women lucky enough to live in a 'safe' area, the war, from its exciting September 3, 1939 beginning, complete even with the fearful frisson of an air-raid warning false alarm, brought the stirring thrill of the prospect of 'something different' happening every day. In some cases – but not in Win Inkster's – there was the hope, sometimes the happening, of a new love, once the buff OHMS envelope had called away the husband.

When it was all victoriously over, Win became bored with the motionlessness of Peace, so she took a part-time job in a nearby factory and saved up every year for a package tour of Europe. At first she went by coach, but eventually became brave enough to try air travel. She purposely returned very sun-tanned to show off to all the neighbours.

Johnny described his father, Lance, as 'A large fat police sergeant in the local Barkingside nick'. He enjoyed the war, too, as he was too old to be called up, and anyway had varicose veins from doing point duty in his early days in North London, down what he called Seven Blisters Road and Manor House Point where there was a large crossroads with no traffic lights in the 1930s. Dad enjoyed fishing and shooting – he had several sporting guns – and he shot rabbits on local farms to help out the meat ration. His politics, according to Johnny, were to the right of Attila the Hun.

'In the mid-fifties he kept half a dozen pigs on a nearby farm, so that helped to fire my interest in farming,' said Johnny in a reminiscing moment. 'He spent a lot of his time dreaming… But Dad never swore, drank, gambled or smoked.'

The remainder of Johnny's family were two older sisters about whom he knew or seemed to care little. Cynthia, taking after Dad, became a policewoman. The more academic Joyce spent three years in college then became a teacher.

The family home in Hainault was newly built and 'really posh', according to the young son. 'Dad bought it in 1938. The cost price was four hundred and ninety-five pounds, but he had a mortgage, of course. One pound down to start it off. Mum used to brag about the house, especially the two toilets – one upstairs and one down. That made it for her; something to tell the neighbours about. We also had two gardens, one front and one back. And a side entrance to the garage. Not many people had all that in those days.'

Anxious to make a start in the real world, Johnny left school almost as soon as it was legal. His recollection of the local grammar school where he received such formal education as he could assimilate was 'good school, poor pupil'. Not having been an academic achiever or toiler in any subjects other than cricket and woodwork, early job-hunting proved difficult.

'I liked farming and the farming fraternity. I wanted to be in cattle, but there wasn't enough money. And it was the end of the smallholder time. In the Second World War people had kept their own chickens, and if they had four acres, they could farm in a smallholder way. But in 1957 it was all ending.'

Nevertheless, even before he left school Johnny had embarked upon his favoured career.

'I bought my own first cattle – three calves, six quid, eight quid and nine quid – while I was still at school. Sold them eighteen months later when I left school for one hundred and ten pounds, the three. So I had my first hundred quid! But I never had a job.

'So, how did I get the money to buy the calves? Well, I had rented a small orchard at eight pounds a year. I sold a bushel – 40 pounds – of apples for ten bob a time, so you see it was self-financing. But I guess I must have begun with a shilling or two, so I suppose Dad underwrote me.

'I didn't have any means of transport, so my apple sales were confined to the local village, Chigwell Row. The buyer was the grocer, Jack Shepherd, also known as 'Old Sixer', no one knew why. The grocer's main claim to fame (or shame) was that he was the last soldier of World War I to receive and recover from the drastic Number One punishment of being lashed to the wheel of a field gun that was kept in use at the time. Shepherd's punishment was for desertion, but he had just gone AWOL while in the UK. It was considered – but not stated by whom – that he was mentally unfit to return to the front.'

As one of Johnny's early business contacts, however, he was no problem and a good regular source of early income from sales. It was not too long before the fledgling entrepreneur was planning his next move. Farming was still on his mind. There was a local outfit owned by Unilever manufacturing cattle food under the title 'British Oil and Cake Mills' and he approached them for a job. It was a show farm, where local farmers could catch up with the latest farming methods. Johnny's idea, in around 1958, was that it would be a good place to start work and at the same time learn. 'However,' he said, 'they didn't want me.'

But as time went on the tables would become curiously turned.

By the age of seventeen he had invested thirty-two pounds of his first hundred pounds to rent half an acre of land for a year, on which he reared up to a hundred pigs on 'pig swill' – mainly waste food from fish and chip shops and Chinese restaurants in London's East End. 'I bought a van for five pounds to collect it and brought the swill back to boil it up in a large second-hand boiler. What a stink! I had my first run in with the local council sanitary inspector – what we'd nowadays call Health and Environment. Well, anyway, the council couldn't act, because at that time smells from pigs were not against the law.'

'Feeding pigs on swill was right up my street,' he said, 'especially as it came for free. You couldn't feed cattle for nothing, but pigs, you could. And swill was really good for them. It wasn't just muck. It had all the healthy ingredients they could thrive on. The minerals they needed were in the fish bones. There was chicken meat a-plenty in the Chinese scraps, beneficial oils in the fried stuff, and vegetables galore! They loved it.'

The Chinese community in the East End dockland area was just beginning to open up its restaurants and these soon became popular eating places even for the toffs and business people from London's West End. Every Chinese restaurant at that time was run by a Chinese family group who lived and slept on the restaurant's upper floors. They produced so much waste that before long borough councils eventually placed 'swill bins' on street corners for the benefit of local pig farmers.

But before Johnny could take his five-pound van to do the regular swill-collecting trips he had to acquire a driving licence.

'Of course I thought it would be a piece of cake,' he admitted. 'I'd had lots of experience driving tractors and farmer's jeeps and trucks, but only off the road. So a couple of weeks before my seventeenth birthday, I applied for a provisional driving licence, which at that time included lorries. At the same time I applied for a driving test. There was a waiting list.

'I considered myself a competent driver, expert even. After all I had often driven – with Dad next to me – in my five quid Trojan 7-cwt van with its two-stroke engine with two cylinders, similar to what you would find in a lawn mower today. Its steering was mechanical, worn out and all over the place. The steering wheel was sloppy and had to be turned a considerable way before anything happened. Every bump or stone jerked the steering and the wheel would fly out of your hand – you had to grip tight and use all your muscles to keep the car on the road. Brakes were mechanical and worn and pulled up each wheel at different times, resulting in uneven braking and a heart-stopping event each time you pushed the pedal down. Advance planning was the order of the day where braking was concerned.

'Anyhow, I reckoned if I could drive that, I could drive. As the test would tell.'

Naturally, Johnny planned to take his test in his own vehicle. After all, he was proud of his van, especially because it was similar to the Brooke Bond tea van, familiar to thousands who fondly watched the first TV adverts. He felt his van had a touch of fame about it.

But Johnny's hopes were dashed on the day of his test when a friendly garage owner announced with some authority that no examiner would get into the van, let alone be driven in it by a learner. He offered a car from his forecourt stock for Johnny's test.

'I chose a Morris Minor and the first time I drove it was on the way to the centre in Ilford. I thought I was wonderful, but it seemed the examiner didn't agree. I blamed it on the fact that I didn't know the car. Never mind that I had no idea what to do at a junction. But to my surprise and disappointment, he failed me just the same. I guess the reality was he could see I couldn't drive.'

To achieve a driving licence eventually, Johnny borrowed a friend's ancient Ford to practise on until the day his next test came up. He had an additional bit of luck this time on the venue. A new centre had just been opened in Loughton where the newly acquired examiner was a retired policeman, a chum of his Dad's who had once served under him in the force. Nothing was said between the two old mates, not even a nod, but after a verbal test on the Highway Code and a ten-minute drive down the road, Johnny gained his licence. 'That inspector was obviously a man who could recognise a good driver when he saw one,' Johnny grinned.

While the hundred pound calves and the hundred pigs, the orchard and the half-acre were the foundation of Johnny the Farmer, it was the purchase and operation of the van that caused the brilliant brain to figure the first fumbling steps towards that desired million mark.

'It was like this: I had to find a way where my transport could earn its keep both ways, if you get me. There had to be some way of getting paid for collecting in it, and payment for delivery of the same stuff. Travelling with an empty van was a waste of money.

'But before I solved that problem, I bought a better van, then a lorry, and formed a private company with one hundred one pound shares. Seventy-five percent was owned by me, twenty-five by my father. The new van had a sign written on the side saying: *John Inkster Ltd* followed by the word *Farmer*. That achieved two important things. The first was that other farmers would be more likely to trust me, being one of them. And the other, more important, factor was that the vehicle – and any others I might acquire in the future – could be taxed as a farmer's vehicle which was exempt from lorry tax and I was issued with an F licence which was about a quarter of the cost. The vehicles were to be used only for the farmer's own use, or carrying goods for his farm. But, as time went on, there were ways and means....

'Sometimes in quiet moments I would wonder about what I was going to do next,' Johnny remembered. 'Farming was fine, and I loved it – but I could see that it wasn't a big money job. Some of the blokes I knew in the business who had large farms and were not short of the odd bob had inherited the land and the farm. Clearly, it wasn't going to be like that for me. My dad's farm was only a smallholding.

'While I was contemplating on this subject I met up with a man called Percy Beaumont.

'We met when I sold him a load of hay for his cow. And over the deal we got talking. He was in the wood business one way and another. He had a timber mill and a wood merchants in Stratford E15 where he imported timber and there was sawing and planing going on there for the East London furniture trade.

'He gave me – gave, because he wanted to get rid of them quick – my first load of chippings... one hundred sacks.'

Now, everybody who has ever been to a circus knows that there is a great familiar association between sawdust and wood chippings and the running of a circus, so Johnny took his first vanload of chippings to the appropriately named Chipperfield's Circus, and sold those first hundred sacks for sixpence a sack. It was not a fortune, but it was the inspiration and the beginning.

Percy Beaumont had several yards to clean up and introduced Johnny to other timber yards and mill owners around the district. Within a month Johnny had purchased a larger lorry that could carry two hundred sacks and he was able to do two or three loads a day. A bigger lorry meant he could supply bigger farms with the sawdust they needed for battery hen houses and bedding for animals, so the price went up, first to ninepence a sack, then to a shilling. In good times he could make as much as thirty pounds a day, six days a week. ('We worked Saturdays then,' explained Johnny.)

The new larger vehicle and the gradually increasing trade now seemed to him to be the beginning of a flourishing business, so he decided to sell his remaining cows and pigs and with the money bought another large lorry. Doug Lock, his cowman helper, was now metamorphosed into a lorry driver. 'I trained him myself,' Johnny confessed. 'My method was to let him drive and if he looked like he was getting into trouble, I just jabbed him with a stick. When I thought he was ready, I arranged his test at Loughton, hoping we might get Dad's old mate.

'Now when Doug was stressed, he stuttered. More stress, more stuttering. We took Dad along and we were lucky; Doug was fortunate that Dad's chum was there. But, even then, not everything went right. For instance… Doug politely opened the lorry door for the examiner and… what happened? Only for an oil filled hydraulic jack to fall out and it weighed about thirty pounds – and it fell on the examiner's foot. This upset him somewhat. Also, the jack had leaked oil all over the lorry floor and during the test ran all over the examiner's shoes! Doug had already stammered his way through the Highway Code test, stuttering so badly the examiner couldn't understand most of the answers. The road test was so quick it was obvious to me that Doug had failed but he was told by the examiner he had passed. I just got a glimpse of Dad and his friend having a chat. I don't know what it was about but they were both laughing conspiratorially.'

Both vehicles were licensed to *John Inkster Ltd, Farmer* as before and were issued with F licences. Whenever queried, Johnny's plausible argument was that the chips and sawdust were used only for his own animals and that any surplus, which of course he had not bought, was passed on to other farmers, sometimes for a small fee. If Johnny and Doug should ever be stopped by the police for any suspected traffic offence, the copper was shown that it was 'F' registered and carried only woodchips. As Johnny knew from his father's life in the police force, a copper would rarely question further, especially as it would be likely to cause all sorts of complications for himself and extra work including tedious form-filling back at the nick.

Johnny ran his lorries like this for several years, and indeed sometimes even 'forgot' to tax either his or Doug's vehicles. He knew Doug could be relied upon, if questioned by an inquisitive policeman, to reply: 'It's in the post, governor.' Then Johnny would have to make a quick visit to the taxation office in Chelmsford and tax the vehicle over the counter, usually back-dating the application by one month.

Johnny's view of those who worked for motor taxation offices was not exactly flattering: 'I reckon,' he would say, 'they have to have special qualifications to be employed there. They all have to be bloody miserable and male or female wear those thick bottle-glass lenses in their specs. They are specially trained to process the forms as slowly as possible. And their big delight is to find some small imperfection in the form the vehicle owner's filled in. Then the poor sod, who's already queued for an hour to get there, is gleefully sent away to re-do his application at a desk right at the back of the hall, then queue up all over again.

'At a cost of several million pounds a new taxation office was built in Stratford E15 to serve the East London and West Essex catchment area. Well, it turned out to be the same as Chelmsford. Same miserable and unhelpful staff dealing with the permanent long queue of people waiting to tax their cars and lorries.'

One day Johnny was stopped by a policeman who noticed his tax disc was out of date, and warned that he would be reported for this offence. As always, Johnny was in a hurry but decided a delay today was better than a fine tomorrow, so slipped home, in between journeys picking up another load of chips, to collect his logbook, insurance certificate and a cheque, then he nipped in to the Stratford office on his way for the next load. He looked in dismay at the lines of people yawning through the hours they had to wait. Sixty or seventy deep at the desk where – all being well – you presented your request and the money and collected your disc. But, alas, before that you had to pick up an application form, fill it in – and the dozen or so applicants who had collected their forms were now lined up to await the use of one of the only available pens with which to complete the job.

Johnny knew that if he queued he would miss the load he had promised to pick up and thus miss half a day's work and its pay; but if he didn't pay the tax, he'd be summoned. And only God and the beak would know how much time would be wasted in court.

While debating his next step, he spotted the son of a local pig farmer half way up the main queue so Johnny, armed with a blank form and his documents greeted him with a plea: 'Hello, Sid, let us in with you?'

'Bugger off,' said his friend. 'I've been here nearly an hour. Get to the back, yourself.'

Faced with such an amicable response, Johnny could do nothing but turn to the back of the queue.

However, as he turned round he spotted a door marked 'Manager' and without quite knowing what his next move might be, he plucked up his courage to knock at the door.

A voice called 'Come in,' and in the split second it took him to enter, Johnny knew what he was going to try. A stern-looking gent sat at a desk. 'Yes?' he queried with a frown. 'What do you want?'

Johnny put on his most humble act, resembling, he hoped, Dickens' Oliver Twist asking for a second helping. 'I'd like a little help, please...'

Seeing the blank form in Johnny's hand, the manager made a guess: 'Ah. Well, all the instructions are on the back, it's quite easy...'

'Yes, but you see, I can't read or write. I can only sign my name. And I need a farmer's licence.'

As not many people farmed in Stratford, this was a new experience for the manager – a farmer crawling to him for help. His attitude eased and he took Johnny's logbook and insurance to inspect it.

When he saw the word 'Farmer' on the logbook, he called in a female assistant.

'Complete this form,' he ordered her, and while he read out to Johnny the questions such as: date, address, weight of lorry and so on, the girl filled in the blanks. Johnny signed it and waited a moment or two while the manager took it round the back of the counter, picked up the disc, put a rubber stamp on it, the girl completed it, gave it Johnny. They all smiled, shook hands, and Johnny left. In and out in about ten minutes.

The son of his pig farmer friend had only progressed about a yard, so as Johnny passed him on his way out, he waved his tax disk, gave a V sign and was away in plenty of time to pick up his second load.

Industry, in this business, he decided, was not enough. You needed guile as well.

When Johnny sold his herd of a hundred pigs to buy a larger lorry, he thought he had finished with the porcine family forever, but it seems that pigs had other ideas.

One day when he was delivering the usual supply of wood chippings to the Chipperfield circus, he met up with one of the young animal trainers.

'You'll never guess what I've been doing this morning,' the trainer greeted him.

Johnny was wise to the sometimes seriously eccentric ways of circus folk, and was not, therefore, prepared to make a guess. After all, it could be anything from giving an elephant a shave to playing a game of chess with a baboon. So, 'No idea, mate,' was his reply.

'Been teaching three little pigs to pirouette on their hind trotters.'

'You what?' exclaimed Johnny, although he was not as surprised as he pretended. 'How in the name of Zoology do you start to do that? What's your method?'

'Well, I began by talking encouragingly to them. Sometimes then I have to give them the occasional sharp tap on the rump. I've even tried kindness,' he joked.

'Are you getting anywhere with them?'

'Oh yes. They're already proper little prima ballerinas.'

It wasn't long after this conversation that there were paragraphs in the local papers, and coloured advertisements on the hoardings about 'The Unique Performing Piglets'. And, shortly after that, Johnny's father, Police Sergeant Lancelot Inkster (known as 'Inky' to his colleagues) heard about the pirouetting pigs, although not from his son. He was informed about this 'dreadful cruelty' from a local animal-loving female busy-body who came into the police station clutching a handful of cuttings and a poster, protesting and demanding that 'something must be done'.

After studying the evidence, Sergeant 'Inky' explained gently that, as far as he knew, there was no law against training animals to dance; then, as he noticed the busybody was opening her mouth to make further protests, added tactfully that he would give the matter some further thought and research and would see if anything could be done. As soon as the lady had departed, he gave the matter no further thought. But, as coincidence would have it, he was reminded of the Chipperfield pigs within the week, when he was officially informed about a serious outbreak of swine fever in the area, which completely restricted all pig owners from moving their animals. It was his duty, therefore, to send one of his uniformed colleagues to the circus's quarters to inform them that it was now impossible, indeed illegal, for them to send their unique pirouetting piglets touring the country with the rest of the performing animals.

Johnny heard all about this disruption to circus plans, not from his policeman father, but from his trainer friend the next time he made a sawdust and chippings delivery. It was a sad story. Now deprived, for no one knew how long, of their chance of stardom, it appeared the piglets were bottom of the circus fan-club list.

'What will happen to them now?' Johnny was anxious to know.

'Well, I guess no circus likes to have animals around that can't earn their keep. So, it seems we shall just have to let them go off to fend for themselves as best they can in the open countryside.'

'You mean they'll just be chucked out?'

'Yep, that's about the size of it.'

'Would the circus sell them?'

'I guess so, if they got a fair offer.'

'What would be a fair offer?'

22

The young trainer scratched his jaw. 'Dunno. They wouldn't be worth much without me. Nobody else could make them dance.'

Johnny, who could never resist a bargain, jumped in with an offer: 'How about a fiver each?'

'I'd have to ask the powers that be. Hold on a sec. There's one of the bosses over there.'

In a short time, the deal was done. Fifteen pounds in cash changed hands, and the three piglets were smuggled into the back of Johnny's van.

It was the dream of Johnny, and also the hope of all who heard about his rescue of the circus piglets, that he would in time be able to revive their dancing ability, and perhaps put them on at local parties or fetes. But nothing he could do seemed to remind them of their earlier training. When he played a little gramophone rendering of what sounded to Johnny like pirouetting music, they just stood looking at him as though they had never been introduced. So, in the sad end, after feeding them with pig swill until they became too tubby to dance, and when the swine fever restrictions were ended, Johnny somewhat reluctantly decided they had to go.

In sorrow he approached Walls, whose firm, famous for bacon and sausages, was not far away and sold the no-longer pirouetting pigs for £28 each. A neat profit of £69 for his trouble.

After thirty years of policing, Johnny's father was nearing his retirement age. He was looking forward to it with a mixture of anticipation and foreboding. In the Barkingside nick he had been virtually the boss as Sergeant Inky. There were a couple of younger sergeants, to whom he taught his job as well as their own, so that he could pass various tasks onto them and take things easy himself, spending most of his day sitting in the most comfortable armchair by the coal fire, with his carpet-slippered feet resting on the over-mantle, while he read the latest issue of *The Farmer and Stockbreeder*. It was a non-taxing, but sometimes interesting, sort of job.

He supposed he actually enjoyed his work at this, his final station. Barkingside was a country station and there were even sometimes incidental, off-the-record 'perks', especially in the rationing days that continued several years after the end of the war. There were rabbits, for example.

Roy Knott, one of his young PCs who was also one of the station's motor-cyclists, was detailed to do (unofficial) night duty which consisted of procuring, with the aid of a shotgun, rabbits and hares for the other PCs on the relief that night. The sergeants on duty at the time were not generally in the know. Roy's motor-cyclist's coat had large side pockets, which could each house a shot rabbit. One night, however, he managed to bag three rabbits, so two of them were bundled into the same pocket.

As vehicle driver he had to sign off at 0600 hrs on the register in the Station Sergeants' office. At that time there were three sergeants on duty and as he was signing the book, the observant Inky leaned across the counter to hiss in Roy's ear: 'Knotty, tuck that rabbit's foot back in your pocket. And, by the way, you can shoot a pair for me tonight.'

One of Sergeant Inky's favourite pastimes was talking – usually about farming. Like many country people during the rationing period he had his own smallholding, mainly of pigs and chickens, and so had PC Knott, so their similar interest formed a kind of bond between them that was more helpful to Inky than to Roy Knott, who often found his own plans upset by being roped in to perform chores for the sergeant. He even, on one occasion, had to go to assist in the search for a missing pig that had fallen out of the back of Inky's old 5-cwt Ford van, the back doors of which were tied with string which broke when climbing a steep hill. It took them six hours of stumbling through rain and muddy fields before they finally recovered the pig. And police uniforms in those days had no rubber boots or protective clothing.

Sergeant Inkster was only too aware that retirement would not be the same. It might offer him the opportunity of collecting, from the markets in the locality, what he hoped were treasures and everyone else dismissed as rubbish. He would dream of becoming a bit more of a real farmer than the part-time smallholder he now was. But for all his hoping, dreaming and planning, the reality when it happened was nothing like that.

When the time came for him to take his carpet slippers home, and peel off his uniform for the last time, it came as an unpleasant jolt that he had nothing to do.

It was true that he hadn't done much during his days at the nick, but he could train the younger ones, and give orders to the lower ranks. All he could do now was to sit by his home fire, remembering the days when for eight hours in any day he and his team dealt with cases ranging from murder (there were four in his time) to indecency a-plenty, gambling, and illegal lotteries. He recalled how he told the handful of PCs, or one of the other young sergeants what they had to do and how to go about it, while he sat in his carpet-slippers manning the office with the reserve PC, a disabled veteran, who dealt with the telephone.

Retirement, he – like many a man of his age – discovered was not what he had hoped for or dreamed of. It was just one day leaning on the next, with nothing happening; nobody to talk to about the things he wanted to talk about. Nowhere to go. No compulsion to move further than his physical needs demanded. Nothing, it seemed, was worth his while or energy to do or create. No one to tell how they could help, even if he knew how himself. It was a dreary do-less, then do-nothing existence; living and partly living.

Eventually, in a way that he had never visualised nor expected, his salvation came from his son, Johnny.

London's East End at that time had enclaves teeming with émigrés from many countries of the world where either they were not wanted, or did not want to stay.

Now in London, they were struggling to revive the trades and talents that they had brought with them from Germany or Middle-Europe when escaping certain death in Hitler's concentration camps. Some became tailors or factory-hands. Many of the Jewish fraternity took to making furniture as they had in their native land. It was this group that eventually interested Johnny most.

'From somewhere I'd heard that furniture-makers in the course of their work accumulate quite a pile of sawdust and wood chippings,' the young thinker began. 'It's obvious, innit? And, if there's too much of the stuff kicking around, they can't carry on their creating. It's got to be taken away. So….'

Chapter Two
Father's Day

It didn't take long for Johnny to figure out that there must be a way of getting paid for clearing out the wood chippings and sawdust from the factories of those people who didn't want it accumulating because it was a fire risk – sawdust being self-combustible. Taking it away for free was against his business principles.

His friend Percy Beaumont, the East End timber merchant, showed him the way. When his own yards were fully cleared, Percy generously introduced the ambitious young man to the Jewish community of the area who were busily engrossed in the fashioning of furniture – some of it work-a-day stuff, some top class. But in all the small areas, or 'sweat-shops' they controlled there was a constant requirement for the detritus of their trade to be removed from the frequently clogged up hoppers it had been vacuumed into. And since their need was often and urgent, Johnny decided the job was worthy of a fee – so much a sack. However, it was not an easy assessment to make because there were at least eight other competitors regularly sweeping up the woodchips and sawdust, which they were supplying to factories for heating, or sawdust to the fur trade for cleaning pelts.

'It was a day-to-day business, charging fees as often as possible, but what with the competition and no fixed rules, it was a matter of stealing the other chap's suppliers and customers before he stole yours,' the embryo trader confessed. 'We even cleared several for free if they were nice white soft woodchips, but we charged for the hard ones of teak and mahogany, oak and beech because the farmers were not so keen on them as they were dusty. However, they even took them in winter because they were from kiln-dried timber, which absorbed water better. So we had a seasonal market for them, and charged to clear them, of course. Plus collecting for supply and delivery to the farmers at the other end.'

Johnny's frequent incursions into East London's furniture factory area of Hoxton Square, Hackney Road, Bethnal Green Road, Orchard Place, Old Ford Road and Lea Bridge Road only partly met the 'master plan' of having his vehicles carrying paid-for loads both ways. Yes: fine when the furniture people paid up, but not so good when they were swept for free. Also, the lorries had to return empty from farm to East End for the next load. That was against Johnny's principles.

One sunny day, however, came the Grand Solution. John Fowler, a friendly Romford farmer, was in trouble. There was a strike of transporting lorries and he had to get his vegetables to his stall in Spitalfields Market early every morning. Johnny, with his 'farmers' lorries, all personally owned, therefore not on strike, came to the rescue. He agreed to load up the vegetables in the evening for the next day's market, where for six days a week and for nine pounds a load 'going up', he delivered to Spitalfields at four in the morning, and collected sawdust and chippings from the nearby timber yards or furniture factories, which earned him twelve pounds, 'going down'. He delivered the sweepings to sell to local farms before picking up the next vegetable load. It was the perfect beginning of his dreams.

Of course, all was not milk and honey and money in Johnny's life. There were the odd problems, too. Empty sacks, for example, to leave at the mills for filling were always a problem. The cost of new hessian sacks was prohibitive and even second-hand ones were costly. And the wastage was tremendous; a sack could be used only three or four times before it was lost, or stolen or just worn out, so continuous replacements accounted for probably the largest expense of the firm.

Apart from purchase, there were various ways of acquiring these valuable commodities. You could buy them from farmers or from local sack merchants, or you could pinch them from farmers who had empty sacks awaiting collection from other woodchip merchants who had delivered previously. Of course that was a two-way traffic because other merchants pinched your empty sacks. So, something had to be done.

To provide a solution, it was Johnny's idea to buy a van for touring the farms regularly and picking up the sacks as soon as they became empty. The vehicle chosen for this special job was not up to much, chosen because of the firm's precarious financial position. It was a new Austin Mini and cost six hundred pounds, after bargaining with a local dealer.

Johnny's father, Lance, had by now been retired some time from his job with the police. Retirement did not suit him and the family was beginning to worry that he would gradually waste away if something didn't turn up to interest or amuse him and lift him out of his present perpetual lethargy.

His son was aware of the problem and when he bought the Austin van and needed someone to put in charge of the sacks Johnny mentioned the prospect one evening to the old man, whose eyes lit up and his hands trembled with excitement when he was told he was offered and was about to be given the job of driving the van around the Essex countryside to collect sacks from the farms as soon as they were emptied, then take them up to the East End factories, mills and timber yards and drop them off ready for re-filling. A secondary sideline of this important job was to try to get renewed orders from the farmers.

The whole idea was a winner. The van was ideal for the job, fast and nippy, and carried about three hundred sacks, which would keep a mill out of trouble until Johnny could pick up the full load. Also, Lance enjoyed the job. It took him out and about in the countryside, he could spend a pleasant hour or two yarning with the farmers and he could use the van for himself to visit one of his daughters and grandchildren who lived on the west side of London.

There were times, however, when his personal visits overran his work schedule and if he was late arriving with the empties, he got what he called 'a rollicking' from the factory foreman, which wounded the pride of the ex-copper somewhat. But apart from those rare occasions, he loved his new job and the importance and independence it brought him.

It was not unusual on a Friday for him to go out early in the morning, and if the mills were well equipped with empties, and his order book was full, he would 'disappear' for several hours. He would slide off, like an errant child, without telling anyone, to Chelmsford cattle and livestock market where he was always at his happiest. Sometimes he would buy a few chicks, or ducks or a pen of rabbits for his back garden, but most often he would be found among the 'dead stock' looking over old bicycles, lawn mowers, second-hand timber, where these and other useless items could be bought for a few shillings when they came under the hammer.

When he'd changed his early career from farmer to trader, Lance's young son often bought or was given odd bits of machinery or timber from the East End factories he visited for sawdust and wood chips. He would take them on a Friday to Chelmsford market where, if sold, the proceeds would help with wages and other incidentals. When Lance's newfound Friday freedom took him to Chelmsford, Johnny had to give up his own small fry trading there, as his dad would often come home with the junk Johnny had just sold off.

This two-way traffic was not profitable to the main business, especially as Lance was using company cheques to pay the market auctioneer. However, apart from this relatively unimportant hiccup, the employment of his Dad was a success. Lance never took any wages, just drew a few small expenses plus petrol for his private use, and with his help the wood chip business ran a lot more smoothly and the sack problem lessened but did not completely vanish.

There were days, for example, when no matter how hard the old man worked, he could not keep up the sack empties with the production of chips and sawdust. This was mostly in summertime, because then the farmer's requirements were not so great, and the various factories Johnny supplied with wood-chips for heating were not requiring the material to keep their workers warm, although at the same time, the furniture makers were at their busiest turning out their wares, making more sawdust.

One day during summer, Johnny had several telephone calls from one mill or factory after another, yelling out for more sacks. Question: Did his Dad have a vanload he could deliver straight away? Ah, but the problem was finding Dad. Johnny first phoned the family home to speak to his father, but his Mum, Win, answered. No, sorry, Lance had left some time before and as far as she knew was off on his rounds collecting empties from only he knew where. Presumably, if he followed his usual pattern, he would head for London as soon as he had a load and would be delivering the empty sacks to the mills

31

and factories around eleven o'clock. But by midday, several of the factory foremen were on the blower to Johnny again, screaming for the sacks. Dad had obviously not turned up, so all Johnny could do was apologise and say that no doubt the sacks were on their way.

By one o'clock there were still no empty sacks and more and different foremen were on the phone, desperate for somewhere to put their accumulating debris.

Now more puzzled than worried, Johnny phoned home again to Mum to find if she had heard anything from her husband, perhaps he'd had a breakdown, or a puncture, Johnny reasoned. But no; nothing. No news. So his next move was to phone round to several of the farmers along the route he guessed Lance would have taken that day. The answer was still the same. No one had seen or heard from him. It was not a Friday, so there would be no market in Chelmsford for him to visit. Where was he, then?

Three o'clock and still no sign. Four o'clock and there was a desperate call from one of the factories. They had had to close down their planing machines as there were no sacks and the huge piles of chips were blowing all over the place, so the workmen had been sent home early. Johnny, anxious to do something – anything – to solve the problem, went to a sack merchant and bought in several hundred more, piled them in his truck and set off to London with them. But, of course, it was after five o'clock by the time he got there and the working day was gone.

By now everyone – Johnny, his Mum, the mill and factory foremen and owners, Johnny's driver, Doug, and the farmers – was speechless with anger because owing to the lack of sacks, there would be only part loads coming to them the next day. It was now seven o'clock and still no word.

By nine o'clock, Johnny's anger turned to anxiety. Where the hell was the old man? Since there had been nothing from him at all, Johnny now concluded that there must have been an accident and, if so, surely they would soon hear. After all, the van had his name and telephone number sign-written on its sides, and the vehicle would have contained papers of various sorts giving the company address. Yes, the police would let them know soon.

By midnight, still with no news of Lance or from the police, Win decided there and then that the only answer was that her husband had decided to leave home. He wasn't a drinker, so that was the only solution and she was sure that, therefore, there was nothing further anyone could do.

The next morning at about eight o'clock after a sleepless, worrying night, Johnny's telephone rang. It was Dad.

'Where the hell are you?'

'At home.'

'Where the devil have you been?'

'When?'

Johnny's patience was evaporating, 'Yesterday, of course.'

'Oh,' his father replied. 'Well, it was like this... I was going along the A12 to collect some sacks, when I saw a sign to the Dartford Tunnel. As you know, it goes from Essex under the river into Kent. And I thought to myself: it's a tunnel I've never been through, so I'll give it a try. When I came out the other side, they charged me a toll, so I thought, well, since I've spent half a crown to come to Kent, I might as well see some of it. It was a lovely sunny day. I hadn't motored many miles when I saw a sign to Pegwell Bay and the Hovercraft near Ramsgate, and it said you could get to France in thirty minutes.

'Well, I'd never ever even seen a hovercraft, so I followed the signs to Pegwell Bay, and I paid my money and went over to Calais. It was a lovely day in France, too, so I spent the rest of the day there and caught the last hovercraft back and arrived home just a bit after midnight.' He gave a happy little sigh at the memory.

Johnny was flabbergasted. 'What about the bloody sacks?' he yelled, 'Half London is at a stand-still.'

'Oh, it's all right,' soothed the old man. 'I'll do them today.'

'But what can I tell the mill owners? And the furniture factory managers? What shall I say?'

'Just tell them I went for a day out in France.'

Johnny held his aching head. 'They'll never believe me. Never.'

When things eventually got back to normal, and the familiar sight of this six-foot-two, sixteen stone driver of a Baby Austin piled high with sacks was seen back on the road again, the firm's mascot that he had become was forgiven by farmers and mill owners alike, because – well, because he was a character.

Another man was to become important in Johnny's life. He was also a character, but one of a totally different calibre. He met him first as a customer for a simple load of hay for the single cow he kept in the garden of his Essex home. Then, as their friendship developed, Johnny realised that here was a man, similar in some ways to himself but, being older and more experienced, could provide him with some of the keys to the success he craved, that this man had achieved and that his own father was unable to supply.

Chapter Three
Philosophy of Shortages

Percy Beaumont had a sneaking admiration for the young Johnny. He liked the spirit of enterprise; the ambition and the ability to both work and think. And at the same time, Johnny liked the older man – in fact he slightly envied the lifestyle that he had worked to achieve for his family.

If ambition plus example were the spur to a young man hoping for success, Johnny had plenty of both. He had his own overwhelming ambition, and the hopes of his father for him.

And now came the example of the man he called Perce. Percy Beaumont had been much like Johnny in his youth and now he and his wife, Joan, could enjoy the fruits of their earlier hardships and endeavour.

Percy had spent some years in the RAF, first as an aircraft fitter on the King's Flight and eventually, during the war, rising to the rank of corporal. Any spare time he could find he used fashioning toys out of wood. He made a windmill with sails that turned; a little wooden walking man; a duck that flapped its wings when it was pulled along; and a series of wooden toy aeroplanes.

There were few toys available for the war babies, indeed with his ear to the ground, Percy learnt that a local famous toy manufacturer had been taken over for the production of munitions, so with his mind on the chance offered by shortage, he took his models home to Forest Green on his weekend leaves and Joan painted them then wheeled them to nearby toy shops or sold them direct to parents for their toddlers.

After demobilisation Percy, realising that commercial property came cheaper than residential, decided to buy a shop with a flat above, as it provided a workplace plus domestic quarters. He spent the cold winter of 1947 cutting and selling firewood to provide money for his family.

Good wood for fires was rationed then, so he chopped his bundles from timber scraps gleaned from London's blitz areas.

As time went by he purchased a series of similar properties, the family living upstairs, the shop floor being used for the sale of all types of timber off-cuts and over-runs sold to anxious builders searching for the materials they needed for the rebuilding or repairing of London's blitzed properties. Percy never worked there, he rented a timber mill and a couple of years later acquired a larger one.

He was not the sort of man to brag about his financial position to others, but he was soon able to pat his back pocket and say to himself: Eight hundred pounds in there for a rainy day.

The rainy day came with the purchase price of a pick-up truck, essential for the transportation of timber. As all timber was rationed at that time and hard to come by – another shortage to cash in on – he collected bomb-damaged wood from London's badly blitzed East End and began a thriving business while the capital was being rebuilt.

Eventually he opened his own timber yard and mill in Stratford and by the time Johnny met up with him, he was making enough money to relax a bit and take regular family holidays in Clacton. By now the flat and workshop had been swapped for the greater comfort and space of a house with garden.

In Clacton he had discovered another shortage to be served. He had noticed that his favourite seaside resort lacked enough small and cheap accommodation for the growing number of summer visitors, so he set about solving the problem by constructing wooden caravans in his garden – he had the wood, and if similar vans were good enough for gypsies, why not for others? – and transported them to Clacton where he rented them out for the holiday season.

The 'philosophy of shortages', as he called it, was one that also appealed to Johnny, and eventually also became his aim. He was sufficiently envious of the success and the methods of the older man that he saw no harm – indeed, saw it only as flattery – in taking some of the ideas and methods to blend into his own life.

He visited the Beaumont home often, sometimes to arrange a pick-up of sawdust and chippings from the Beaumont timber mill in the East End, sometimes to deliver a sack or two of chippings for the Beaumont farm animals, sometimes to chat and peer into the Beaumont mind and sometimes, Johnny had to admit, to admire the two young Beaumont daughters Joyce and Marion.

Joyce, it seemed, was the more serious-minded and too busy concentrating on a career to be bothered just then with boys; Marion was attracted to and dating what her mother described as 'a nice Jewish young man from down the lane'. There was a slight impression hovering in the air that Joan reckoned that the young Inkster was a ne'er-do-well. But, of course, she kept her feelings to herself; her daughters made their own decisions, although she and Percy were always there to see them right should there be any clouds on their horizons.

The irony of the situation was that it was originally through his friendship with the parents of the young man from down the lane that Johnny first heard of the Beaumont family. At the time he was delivering hay for the farm animals of the Jewish family. As it appeared Johnny was a reliable supplier, the farmer suggested that perhaps Percy Beaumont's house cow might also profit from an introduction. Johnny's first meeting with Marion was not a great success. She opened the door to him, hardly noticing this man she immediately assessed as 'old' and then 'a bloody idiot' as he ran his van over her father's ladder, shattering it beyond repair and, in his embarrassment, drove off without a word.

In spite of what her mother may have thought or hoped Marion had no immediate intention of going steady with the young Jewish neighbour, or anyone else at the moment. He was six years her senior and in any case his father was against the liaison because she was a C of E 'goy' girl. She was young enough to enjoy playing the field and going out one night with one date, then the next with some other young man. Staying out, to her mother's disapproval, until 'all hours'. Marion tried to explain that many of those hours were spent simply saying goodnight on the doorstep.

Johnny was not entirely unaware of the attractions of this lovely and lively young lady; she was so popular it seemed that every time he arrived at the Beaumont home, she was just leaving for a date. However, he was philosophical enough to shrug it off and spend the rest of the evening in the congenial company of Percy. After a month or two, however, he thought he would try his luck and he asked Marion for a date.

She refused him then, and several times subsequently, preferring now to be with the ever growing more serious Jewish suitor.

It seemed to Marion that Johnny was always around. He was there when she went out in the evenings and was still there yarning with her father when she returned. 'He seemed to have so many tales to tell about his past and what had happened to him,' she said, 'that I thought he was really old. I just didn't fancy an old boyfriend. It turned out in the end he was only two years older than me.'

Once Johnny Inkster had made up his mind about something, there was no stopping him, and the more he saw of Marion with her lovely long dark hair swinging in what he thought of as a saucy pony-tail, the more he heard her laughter and the more he grew to admire the Beaumont family way of life, the more determined he became to become part of it.

In his mounting desperation Johnny even tried suggesting a double date with Marion, her sister Joyce and a friend of his who was willing to make up a foursome. The ruse nearly worked, but when the three of them arrived to pick up the other young man at his home, he had just received a message from his regular girlfriend, a nurse, saying she was suddenly off duty and was coming round that evening. So Johnny was now stuck in a 'gooseberry' triangle with the two sisters. He valiantly tried to entertain them by taking them to the bright lights of Southend, but the rain came down in torrents and the whole evening was a disaster.

Nevertheless, the evening had proved that Marion was not averse to going out with him, providing he made it interesting enough. So he set about devising amusing and entertaining evenings for their dates. It has long been well known that any personable, handsome, ambitious, sweet-talking young man who is a charming entertainer, who would never bore any audience, could easily turn a girl's head in his direction and wrench her heart away from any other serious suitor. And so it was with Johnny and Marion. The 'nice young man from down the lane' now stood little chance and was, no doubt kindly, dropped.

Joan Beaumont's old mother, Flo, came to live with the family around that time. And Grandmother was as wily as any other member of the family. Whenever asked to do some task she had no intention of carrying out, her reply would always be: 'Yes, all right, I'll get round to it on Michaelmas Day....' Gradually, the family realised that was her encoded message for 'Never'.

The ruse was remembered by Marion and came in handy when she had for the umpteenth time refused to discuss the prospect of an engagement with Johnny.

'All right,' she echoed her grandmother; 'we'll get round to it on Michaelmas Day.'

The excited young man, innocent of the Beaumont code, leapt up, happily embracing the girl; 'That's wonderful. September 29 – Michaelmas Day. That's the day farmer's rents are paid.'

Marion hastily back-tracked a little, resolving never to use her grandmother's excuse again, said: 'Er – well, maybe not next Michaelmas....'

Before the following Michaelmas came, Johnny thought it would be prudent to try to seal the pact, if indeed a pact it was, with at least some talk about an engagement ring.

Marion expressed her desire for a solitaire diamond, whereupon Johnny consulted his bank balance... That would only supply enough for a very small solitaire with only the glimmer of a sparkle. Immediate future prospects didn't look very promising either. Nothing for it, then, but to sell one of the cows from his smallholding.

When that deal was done, and his pocket was bulging with cow money, he consulted a friend – who was a colonel, so Johnny reckoned he must know about such things. The colonel told him the place to go was Hatton

Garden and said he knew a jeweller there who would oblige. So an appointment was made and the couple went 'up West' (as they saw it, although it was actually London EC1) to the street of gem merchants that lies between Holborn Circus and Clerkenwell Road. On their way to the contact they gazed into all the shining shop windows and by the time they arrived at their destination Marion's yearning for a solitaire had somewhat evaporated and when a glittering diamond cluster was produced she held her breath, tried it on and announced to Johnny: 'This is it. This is the one I'd like.'

And so, come the following Michaelmas, there was an engagement party for about a hundred and fifty guests, held in a barn in Percy's garden. Music was provided by Marion's cousin who was drummer in the band of Troy Dante and the Infernos. Marion voted it 'a brilliant party'. Johnny was not so sure, he had bought a new pair of shoes for the occasion and when the music stopped at day break he found he had worn them entirely away dancing on the barn's concrete floor. But they were engaged and had a ring and a party to prove it.

On the sixth of July 1963 the Essex sky was a seamless grey curtain of rain for the whole day and Marion and Johnny were married. It was a posh wedding, according to Marion, at All Saints Church at Chigwell Row. However, before they got as far as walking down the aisle, there was a long period of questions and misgivings, not from the young couple themselves, but from the older members of the family. Marion's mother, Joan, worried about the suitor – no 'proper job', no sign of a regular income, no home to offer his bride. She didn't, however, voice her worries too loud, but mentioned them gently to Percy. Percy, already fond of the young man to whom he had become adviser, prompt and friend, tried to shush away his wife's fears, reminding her that their own beginnings had been almost as risky.

'Yes, but –' Joan interrupted him and pointed out that she had been an able and willing helpmate, while their daughter showed no sign of abandoning the work she loved of running the local dancing school with her sister.

So Percy, probably in favour of 'peace at any price' came to Joan's – and Johnny's - rescue with the offer of a nearby cottage as the couple's first home.

For some time he had been investing in property. His first adventure in that direction had been to buy up a string of second-hand prefabricated bungalows, which in some areas of East London were being taken down. Prefabs had originally been built as a 'temporary solution' to the housing shortage after the war when many London homes had been flattened and the troops returning from their overseas service had nowhere to live on demobilisation until the tide of demolition and reconstruction had taken place. Percy decorated and pebble-dashed the prefabs, re-sited them on the River Blackwater in Essex, an area he and the family knew well, and rented them out. Marion and her mother cleaned them up between lets as the tenants moved in or out.

But it was not one of these the young couple were to have. Instead, just after the engagement, Percy bought a bungalow down the lane, four doors away from 'Zinnia', his own home, and rented it to them for three pounds a week. It was called 'Five Oaks' and had a smallholding of four acres. It was situated in an unmade country lane along with about twenty other properties. These had all evolved after World War I when the land was sold off to smallholders; and slowly metamorphosed in the late 50s and early 60s into homes for various small businesses and their owners. The neighbouring businesses now included a tent manufacturer, a haulage business, a fairground store, and market trader. The bungalow Percy bought to rent to Johnny had previously been owned by an elderly couple, and therefore the place was not in the best state for the first home of a new bride. And Johnny, though willing enough, was not the world's greatest handyman.

'Johnny's knowledge of d-i-y is n-i-l,' Marion complained. 'He probably doesn't even know it means 'do-it-yourself.'' Luckily, she had an uncle who was a decorator by trade and who offered to help out. The house was structurally pretty sound, but there was still a lot to be done, so Johnny knew that his free time from now on was spoken for, at least as an assistant to the uncle.

The winter of 1962-3 had been snowy and record-breakingly cold, and there were insufficient electric points in the house to keep the workers warm and the fireplace smoked badly. In a moment of ignorant enthusiasm, Johnny decided that the chimney needed a clean, so he pushed some sweep's brushes up it. They became so stuck that even the combined efforts of the uncle and Johnny could neither push them further up nor bring them back down. Just in case they did manage to dislodge the brushes, Johnny slammed the door of the room shut so that any resulting dust or soot would be contained in the one place. This may have seemed a good idea but the slamming completely dislodged the handle and it fell to the floor on the other side of the closed door, leaving Johnny with only the knob in his hand. The two men were now imprisoned and had to remain that way for several hours in the freezing room until Joan came to see how the work was progressing and managed to let them out with the handle from her side of the door.

It was probably secretly decided by the members of the Beaumont family that Johnny was not going to be a big help in the numerous tasks that lay ahead to make the bungalow habitable but eventually the sweeping brushes, accompanied by birds' nests, were successfully removed from the blocked chimney. Percy thought he would spend his evenings, when he returned home from his timber mill, installing new electric wiring into the little house. He instructed Johnny in the art of channelling out the walls ready for him to work on later. Ever eager, the young man decided to have a go himself, and added the wires and switches as well. Of course, he had found the channelling right down from the ceiling tedious work so cut the channels shorter than he'd been told and Marion and her father found the switches neatly embedded at about six and a half feet from the floor.

'Oh, I suppose it's because I'm so tall, I didn't notice,' said Johnny when challenged. The same excuse applied when he later erected the mirrored cabinets in the bathroom.

'All very well for him,' Marion sighed, 'but all I could see were my eyebrows.'

Johnny eventually abandoned the indoor work and instead groomed the neglected garden. Borrowing some machinery from Percy, he ironed out most of the humps and bumps and rotovated away the rabbit holes then prepared the whole area ready for spring planting.

By the time the date was set for the wedding, the house was finished and furnished, mostly with gifts, though Johnny did supply the bedroom suite.

The Great Day dawned to black lowering clouds and a continuous downpour of rain, but Marion was not downhearted.

'It was a posh wedding,' she bragged to friends afterwards. 'I wore a long white frocky job with frills down the back going into a train. My bridal bouquet was roses and stephanotis. I had six bridesmaids in pastel colours – two in pink, two in blue and two in lemon. And a page boy in blue velvet and patent leather shoes with silver buckles.'

Johnny asked a friend he much admired, Gordon Hughes, to be best man. Gordon's farm lay alongside the piece of land farmed by Johnny, but it was his daredevil history that most impressed the bridegroom. Gordon had learnt to fly his family's company plane even before joining the wartime RAF where he became a test pilot and subsequently commanding officer of a reconnaissance squadron. He was the pilot who took off in a fog and located the enemy battleship *Tirpitz* sheltering in a Norwegian fjord.

On their way to the wedding, Gordon insisted that he and Johnny walk. It was the right thing to do, he told Johnny, the long trek in the rain to the church in their morning suits would, he stressed, make the bridegroom think of the responsibilities he was about to take on.

After the wedding came the reception, paid for, as is the custom, by the bride's father. Held at the Red House pub in Redbridge, Ilford, it was a jolly affair without any strict formality.

'Well, for example,' Johnny remembered, 'even the speeches were just simple normal ones by Percy, Gordon and me.'

Percy also came to the rescue with the honeymoon. He offered them one of his caravans in Clacton for a couple of weeks. Johnny was not keen; he said he couldn't afford it; he thought honeymoons were a bit of a waste of time and he was anxious to get on with the task of making a fortune at least equal to that of his father-in-law. He had never really fancied a holiday all his life, he said; he didn't see the point. And anyway, the caravan idea didn't appeal. Gordon, his best man and admired friend, strongly disapproved when Johnny mouthed some of these honeymoon horrors and threatened him with a youth hostelling holiday instead. He also gave each of the couple a separate good talking to. He told the bridegroom he suspected he was only marrying into the Beaumont family for money. He informed Marion she should not go ahead with the marriage if it was only because she felt sorry for Johnny. The bond between the couple, however, was too strong to break like this, so it seems that Gordon's warnings had served their purpose. The bride and groom also went together to the Clacton caravan.

As any policeman will tell you, if you have two witnesses you can expect to have two totally different stories. So it was, years later, with the honeymoon memories of Mr and Mrs John Inkster.

Johnny remembers being fed up. 'I don't like caravans. It was summertime and wood chips were hard to sell, so I wanted to get back and get selling.' His business needed him. He recollected the typical East Coast weather – rain blowing off the North Sea. 'As far as I can remember, Clacton was OK, a holiday resort, somewhere I could never afford to go to as a kid. It was my first time there.' His tone implied: '...and the last.'

Marion's romantic memories were quite different.

'We didn't get fed up, but Johnny didn't like it. What happened was he didn't want to go away on honeymoon as he couldn't afford it, but Gordon went berserk and said that attitude was abominable – so we went, thanks to my Dad's offer of a caravan.'

Marion's nostalgic memories of childhood holidays in that resort were hauntingly pleasant. 'Did I like Clacton? Well, it was very ordinary for me as I had been there often as a child and I would have liked it again if I had been given opportunity to enjoy it.

'The weather was lovely. The day we got married it poured. But other than that it was typical July.

'I wondered at first if I would miss my family, especially there, where we had had so many happy holidays together. But I didn't get the chance to miss them. We were only there four days.'

The daily grind of married life was not quite what Marion was used to, nor what she had expected, in that she had no real hard and fast dreams or expectation of what life would be like for her once she had left the darling shelter of her parents' home. She was not of an age or inclination to worry much about her future. She was blessed with the twin virtues of good humour and commonsense, which were among the reasons Johnny had fallen in love with her. It had never occurred to her to wonder whether Johnny was able to keep her in the style to which Percy and Joan had cosseted and accustomed her.

'I suppose I was very naïve.' She later confessed. 'I had never known about not having enough money for things, although we were brought up not to ask and to be grateful for our lot. But I always had enough for a new dress, or shoes or whatever. And my father was a genius. He could, and would, repair anything in the house or garden. He would build or make things for us and I guess we thought that was normal. God, I had a rude awakening. There was very little money, even for the basics. If something fell down or broke it just stayed that way.'

It hadn't occurred to Johnny that apart from his fledgling business and his wits he had little or nothing to offer his bride.

'No,' he admitted; 'I never thought about it. I reckoned you either got married or you didn't, and that was it.'

More importantly to him, now that the honeymoon was over at last, he could get on with his business. In the meantime Marion was contributing to the housekeeping expenses by continuing the popular dancing school she ran with her sister, Joyce. Johnny didn't like the fact that his

47

wife was vanishing from the home two evenings a week and every Saturday morning to teach young people to tread the light fantastic steps or ballet, tap, modern and acrobatic dancing. But Marion was a strong willed young lady and they needed the money.

Johnny was not a great one for discussing money and his financial position, least of all with his young wife. The fact was that at the moment things were not looking too rosy. As a single man it had not really worried him when the farmers told him they couldn't pay until they had taken their pigs to market and found themselves in funds, or the poultry farmers needed credit until they received their pay after the Christmas or Easter feasts. But now he had responsibilities and his time had been lost by the house repairing, the wedding and the honeymoon, plus the fact that in this area, in this year of 1963, it seemed that farming was in the doldrums. Johnny sighed, then shrugged the worries to the back of his mind. Something would turn up, but until it did it was a time for exercising his wit and guile. Of which he had plenty.

The great thing about Johnny's business was that the material you had for sale, wood chippings or sawdust, either came for free or you got paid to take it away. You also got paid for delivery to the farmers; not much, it was true, but at least it was a pretty busy beginning. Your only real overhead expenses were the operating of the team of lorries gradually building up as business expanded. There was then the cost of the lorries themselves, drivers' wages, diesel fuel, and repairs. Johnny was able to withstand quite a bit of credit. Most of his small farmer friends were regulars who paid promptly, either weekly or monthly. It was mostly the larger farming customers who wanted credit. The turkey farmers for the most part wanted to pay only after Easter or Christmas; pig farmers after their pigs had been sent to slaughter.

Because of his frequent dealings with poultry farmers to whom he sold sawdust or chippings for litter, he developed a lucrative side-line by trading in frozen turkeys or chickens which he sold to his London customers whose sawdust he was clearing up.

Some of the big poultry farmers had their own slaughter houses and frozen packing plants. Sometimes the birds were bruised or wounded before they reached the packing department, and could be classed only as seconds and sold off at cut prices. Johnny did a great trade in these imperfect frozen birds sold to his easy-going East End customers, who never asked for a refund when their wives discovered the thawed turkey might have one, or both drumsticks amputated or their chicken might be wingless. After all, the price had been good, so they just laughed, he says, and made remarks like: 'Cor, what a load of cripples!' Or, 'First time we've seen an 'andicapped turkey!'

One large farm on the border of Essex and Hertfordshire had cornfields, milking cows and about ten thousand broiler chickens. Johnny approved of the way these chickens were reared – none of that infamous battery method where the hens were kept tightly cooped up in wire cages just for the production of eggs. This farmer's poultry was reared from day-old to slaughter at about twelve weeks and kept in very large and well-heated and ventilated sheds where they were free to walk around on the wood chip litter. They were being reared for meat rather than eggs.

The farm was run by a very keen first class manager who had been buying wood chips from Johnny for about two years. Payment was not exactly made pronto, perhaps, but there was no real problem; it came along eventually. However, just after Christmas 1963, when Johnny was tussling with the new expenses of being married instead of single, the bottom fell out of the poultry market. Prices had seldom been lower and it seemed nobody wanted broilers. As he had not received the usual payment, Johnny called in on this farm for his cheque only to be told by the manager there was no money for the wood chips. Trade was in the doldrums, he said, however, if a buyer could be found for the chickens, payment would be forthcoming immediately.

'How old are they?' Johnny enquired.

'Twelve weeks,' the manager told him. 'Just ready for slaughter.'

'O.K.' said Johnny. 'Let's have a look at them.'

The chickens turned out to be all cockerels that had been caponised – that is, treated in a similar way to castrating a bull calf to turn it into a bullock so that the animal loses its masculinity, quietens down and puts on weight. Cockerels are not castrated, but a hormone pellet is injected into the neck when they are around six weeks old. The effect is similar, they put on weight, but also it gives them youth, for at twelve weeks they resemble chubby pullets. The price of a point-of-lay pullet is better than a twelve-week caponised cockerel.

After a moment's thought and a good look over the poultry on offer, Johnny agreed to take one thousand of them in lieu of the outstanding bill for wood chips. In fact he had to hand over a small cheque of his own to make up the difference. But he was well satisfied with the deal, particularly the next day, when in conversation with a young Essex farmer, the subject of point-of-lay pullets happened to crop up. The farmer said he was on the look out for some.

Of course Johnny's immediate response was: 'I've got a thousand – very cheap.'

An immediate deal was struck at two hundred and fifty pounds for two hundred and fifty point-of-lay birds, as seen and inspected. As the price was only about two-thirds of the going rate at that time, no guarantee was expected or offered.

A further five hundred were due for delivery to another farmer the following evening. It is always best to transport chickens at night, because when the lights are doused in their new quarters they settle down quickly. On this occasion in particular it certainly suited Johnny's book as in the semi darkness there was less chance of the farmers making too close an inspection of their purchases.

The remaining two hundred and fifty were more of a problem and until it was solved, Johnny had to house and feed them, and that was eating into any profit he hoped to make. Johnny was seldom stuck for an idea, and one day a possible sale of a number of his capons came to him. At Woodford Bridge opposite Claybury police station and next door to Dr Barnado's Home, there was a very old fish shop run by a man called Martin and his wife who gutted the fish and killed chickens. They employed a team of six men and two women who worked in the shop frying the fish and chips, another couple sold wet fish over the counter. The shop was small but always busy because business was brisk. Martin's trade included supplying fish, poultry and game to all the posh restaurants for miles around; the local golf club was another good customer and so were the occupants of the big houses in Manor Road where anyone who had made a fortune in the East End of London came to try to buy a house.

Some of the men employed to work in the yard of the shop, killed about two hundred chickens a day. It was their job also to dip the whole of each dead chicken into a vat of boiling water, and then strip the bird of its feathers by holding it on to the plucking machine. This was like a huge old-fashioned clothes mangle with leather thongs attached to whip around stripping the birds naked.

Johnny had hoped that Martin would have a market for his remaining capons, but business was so bad, Martin had to turn them down. He did, however, offer to kill and pluck them for four pence each. Johnny accepted eagerly, there was always the possibility of offloading them here and there to the East End factory workers when he cleared out their sawdust.

So now he had a load of plucked chickens to dispose of, but at least they didn't need feeding. He put them in the Mini van usually kept for collecting the empty sacks from farmers, and drove up to London with them. These heavy, plump capons at a price way below the present butchers' price, would sell well, he was sure. But it didn't work out like that. It was, unfortunately, too soon after Christmas for many people to fancy another Sunday lunch of poultry again – let alone for a midweek meal.

Now Johnny really had problems. He had no refrigeration facilities for such a huge bulk of birds, and although it was winter, he knew only too terrifyingly well that the raw meat had a very limited time to remain saleable. He decided to leave them where they were in the Mini van, which he locked safely up in his father's garage for the night, while he tried to think of a way out of his trouble. He was not prepared yet to admit, even to himself, that he had really overdone it this time.

'Two days,' he muttered to himself. 'Two days at the most before they go off and begin to smell.'

He had managed to sell only ten or twenty birds since he picked them up from Martin, so the next morning he went off in the Mini to the bank. Not to deposit or draw cash, but to have a quiet word with the manager who, it happened, was quite a fan of Johnny's and had always shown faith in him and encouraged him in his business. So, with a gentle prod from the manager, the bank staff was talked into buying a couple of chickens each for their families. About fifty or sixty capons were disposed of, but of course it was not nearly enough, and back went the remainder into Dad's garage for another night.

That night, Lady Luck – in the form of an Essex winter – came to Johnny's aid. A hard and penetrating frost was the sudden forerunner of a lengthy icy spell. Daylight the next morning brought a temperature well below freezing and the chickens were frozen hard into a solid block of lifesaving ice. For several days the weather showed no sign of thawing and the price of all meat began to rise accordingly. Of course, Johnny's bargain-priced frozen capons became sought after and his sale figures began to rise sharply.

Johnny's willing father was co-opted into delivering the birds around the neighbourhood, and a sign writer who was busy lettering Johnny's new lorry in Dad's garage couldn't understand why the old man kept pushing wheelbarrow loads of frozen hens out of the garage. Eventually, his curiosity got the better of him and he took a peek into the Mini van sharing the garage with the new lorry he was decorating. He was amazed to see a huge tangled mass of frozen fowl and an axe, it was obvious Johnny's father was using to separate them.

The cold spell lasted several weeks, long enough for all the chickens to be sold.

Some weeks later Johnny met the farmer to whom he had sold the first batch of 'pullets' at point-of-lay. To Johnny's surprise, the farmer made no complaint; in fact he seemed unusually and remarkably friendly. Encouraged, Johnny was brave enough, curious enough, to ask how the chickens were doing.

'No eggs, yet,' was the reply, but he continued that they became such lovely big fat fowl that he had killed many of them and sold them off as capons. 'Of course,' he admitted with a wink, 'I didn't mention they were really pullets.'

Johnny was quite pleased with the way he had managed to top up the regular money he made in his sawdust business, and believed that the fact that he met the farmers who had obliged through his day-to-day business made it a sort of allied trade. Perhaps some other opportunity like that one would someday present itself. 'Just a matter of looking out for it,' he told himself'

He did a fair trade with dairy farmers who liked to bed down their cows in individual cubicles where each cow could sleep alone and undisturbed. The tiled floors of these stalls were kept warm and clean by the regular distribution of wood chippings. This also made matters easier for the cowman who had to wash the udders before milking. Dairy farmers seldom kept Johnny waiting for his pay cheque, mainly because such farmers were themselves paid monthly for their fresh milk by the Milk Marketing Board.

But there are exceptions to every rule, and one man who farmed near Epping and milked a herd of some seventy or so was generally a tardy payer. Johnny never knew why. Especially as it was an old family farm for two generations and was known to provide top quality milk, as the main customer was London's Jewish community. This meant that at each day's milking a representative of Beth Din, the authority for kosher foods, had to be present to see that the rules of the religion were adhered to. For this, the farmer was paid a few pence more than the average and the milk was supplied to his Jewish customers via the Milk Marketing Board.

As little or no money had come from this source for a month or two, Johnny decided to pay a visit to his reluctant farmer friend and see what could be done. Perhaps, he suggested, he might buy a cow or some calves from him to 'contra' some of the money owing. The man did not want to part with any cattle, but was shrewd enough to see that such a move was an idea to fob Johnny off until he had some spare funds in a week or two.

'Well,' said the farmer, thoughtfully stroking the side of his jaw, 'I can't part with the cattle, but I'll tell you what... I've a sack or two of seed corn you can have cheap.' He led Johnny into a barn where he indicated several sacks, about four tons in all, of seed for barley and wheat. 'You can have the lot.'

Johnny was immediately suspicious. 'What's wrong with it?' He turned one of the sacks over to inspect it. It was clearly marked as to the variety of the seed. The merchant's name was printed on the sack. And it was also labelled with descriptions of chemical herbicides and pesticides. But it was not dated.

'Come on, Jim. How old is this seed?'

The farmer stroked his jaw again. He didn't want to admit it was beyond its best-before date.

He hesitated, then added: 'Well, I don't think it will germinate too easy. But I thought you could sell it on to a pig farmer for feed corn. It's quite a bargain.'

It certainly seemed it was and Johnny was tempted. He was not one to turn down a bargain. But no actual price had yet been mentioned. And he still had a bargaining point to make.

'No.' he said. 'It's no good for pigs with all those chemicals in it. It'd bump 'em all off.'

'Right,' said the dairyman with sudden determination. 'Take it – all the lot, for twenty-five quid – or leave it.' He was obviously eager to get rid of the stuff anyway and liked the idea of knocking a few quid off his account at the same time.

'Right!' Johnny echoed. His lorry was loaded up and as the two men shook hands the relieved farmer promised to send another cheque soon to further reduce his debt.

As soon as Johnny had unloaded the seed into his yard, he produced a date stamp from his office and stamped each sack with last September's date. He was careful to place the mark at the bottom of the sack where it could hardly be seen, and he blurred the image somewhat as well to make it almost illegible. As the planting season was soon coming up, he wanted to waste no time in ridding himself of his bargain, so that evening he telephoned another Essex farmer who he knew appreciated a good buy.

'Ah, Peter,' he said. 'I've some surplus sacks of barley and wheat you can have for £30 a ton. There's four ton of it. Are you interested?'

'Depends what it's like and how old it is. But I'll come along in the morning and have a look.'

Next day, Peter examined a random sack or two, turning them over to squint at the date, and he seemed satisfied, and said he would take the lot, knowing he was on to a winner. Johnny offered to drop them all off at his farm the next day.

The deal had profited Johnny to the tune of nearly a hundred pounds and would keep the wolf from his bungalow door for a while.

Peter planted all the barley in one of his fields and sold off the wheat to a neighbour. Then came the warming suns of springtime, and as luck –or ill luck – would have it, Peter's barley germinated, sprouted and grew well, but his neighbour was not so lucky with the wheat. His crop was a dead loss, so he complained bitterly to Peter who had sold it to him. Peter, of course, passed on the complaint to Johnny who just shrugged it off, saying that it had never been sold as seed for planting and refused to discuss the matter further, especially as Peter himself had no complaint about the barley.

It was, however, the end of any friendship between Peter and his neighbour who had lost the whole year's production in one of his fields.

A few months later, the farmer gave Johnny his final cheque.

'How did you get on with that seed I sold you?' he asked. 'Did you ever sell it?'

'Oh, sure,' was Johnny's reply, 'next day, no problem.'

Jim laughed. 'I'll bet you killed off someone's pigs.'

'No. I sold it off to a man who thought it was seed corn.'

'Blimey,' said the farmer. 'That must have been old whatsisname, Peter's neighbour. He's been telling the world for weeks how his wheat crop failed him.'

Johnny shook his head. 'Don't know him. I sold him nothing. He must have got some dud stuff somewhere else.'

Chapter Four
Family Business

It doesn't always happen, even in the happiest and best regulated families, that the desire and hopes for the beginning of a family coincide in the minds of Mister and Mrs at the same time. Quite often it is the wife who becomes as broody as a young hen, yearning for an infant's wail to be cuddled away. Sometimes it is the husband whose desire awakens first to a dream of introducing his son into business; to the art of kicking a ball into a goal net, or of stroking the soft blonde curls of a beautiful just-like-her-mother girl child. In another family Mother Nature herself might take a hand and in embarrassment, dismay or dizzy delight the wife discovers the surprise pregnancy.

Johnny and Marion, however, were both planners. Neither liked leaving things to chance, so after a year of getting to know each other, they happily talked things over and scheduled a baby as soon as possible. Johnny secretly hoped it would be a boy, but admitted nothing to anybody. Marion didn't mind, so long as when it arrived it was healthy and had all its working parts.

Realising that the future would soon hold another mouth to feed, another body to clothe and eventually another mind to educate, Johnny began to expand his business and workload. He was so busy he had little time to realise how the pregnancy was affecting his young wife. In any case he had no anxieties about the birth; he was used to dealing with the reproduction of his farm animals and they certainly didn't get or require the medical attention Marion was receiving. Poor Marion's morning sickness did not vanish after a month or two as her mother and girlfriends had said it would.

'It wasn't like that for me,' she remembers. 'It just went on and on and on for the whole nine months.'

Her doctor, an old chap who had guarded the health of the family for three generations, just gently gave the advice he had always given – that there was nothing he could offer to stem the flow. It was just the way things were for Marion and apart from having to put up with the unpleasantness, there was no cause for concern. Marion loved and trusted the old doctor, so decided, in spite of the stories she heard that there were miracle drugs nowadays that could help, she would say nothing, just try to grin and bear it.

And very thankful she later was that her old-fashioned medicine man had probably never heard of the latest wonder drug that so many were prescribing at that time. It was called Thalidomide.

The pre-birth family planning included moving house. The fact was that Five Oaks, the bungalow they rented from Percy, was not really suitable for the advent of a new born. It was a cold house without central heating and, as home births were not the regular thing at that time, it was likely that the health authorities would not allow it to take place where the only hot water available was from a little solid fuel fire with a back burner in the kitchen. As always, the Beaumonts came to the rescue and their darling pregnant daughter and her Johnny moved up the lane to 'Zinnia' the house owned and occupied by Percy and Joan. And Johnny still paid the three pounds ten shillings a week rent.

Nearly everything went according to plan. After almost twenty-four hours of strong and painful labour, the baby's head appeared on schedule in the early hours of Wednesday, March 31. But, as with many births, there was a drama. The baby had gone into distress with the cord causing strangulation by being wrapped three times round the neck. The midwife had to reach in and cut the cord so the child's shoulders could emerge with the rest of him. It was a boy.

'But he's so blue,' Marion cried when she saw him. 'I've never seen a blue baby before. Is he all right?'

She was still alarmed even though when they got him to cry it was announced that he was fine. He kept his blue tinge for a couple more days, then started to become the baby-pink happy and gurgling child Marion had hoped for and expected. Everybody seeing the child remarked how much he resembled his grandpa, Percy.

'You wouldn't believe,' said the new young mother, 'that a tiny baby could look anything like a middle-aged man, but everybody – even Johnny's family – thought so. I did wonder whether Johnny was sort of hurt and would have preferred his son to look like him. But I don't know.'

Johnny's only comment was that he was happy the child was one hundred percent healthy, but he was chuffed it was the boy he'd hoped his first born would be.

Naming the baby caused no real problems. He was going to be named Anthony, a good manly name they all thought, and then Johnny remembered he had once known an Anthony who 'walked funny' and, as that might be an ill omen, how about Mark Anthony? And so he became Mark Anthony with John tacked on, to show whose son he was. Mark Anthony John; nothing wrong with that. Everything right.

'It was around the time of Mark's birth, or not long after,' Johnny later mused, 'that a lot of things began to happen. Percy had recently bought a nearby field of about four acres and was beginning the building of a small house on the land. He didn't immediately say so but I reckoned that his idea was that the house was for us so that we didn't get any idea of moving far away.

'Well, of course I wanted to buy the house, but at first he wouldn't sell. I guess he thought he'd better keep it in case we got divorced. Anyway, I didn't have the money. When Mark was about three months old we moved into the house, which, of course we called The Chippings. And we still paid Percy rent.

'It was a red brick bungalow and was being built by Percy's builders, but when I had time I laboured for them, all the time dreaming of the additions I would make when I owned the house myself.'

Johnny's own father was the cause of a worry or two at the time. Johnny had kept him busy since his retirement by providing him with a Morris Mini van so that he could tour the farming customers, taking orders and collecting sacks to be delivered to the East End factories and mills and while in that area looking around for new mills or furniture factories to approach. These things he did with some initial enthusiasm, but his earlier job in the police force had been one of modest comfort so he had never known the spur that made a man hungry for orders. In any case, his heart was not in it. He was an 'auction-aholic' or treasure hunter and now the wood chip money he had collected would come in handy. He would take off any auction day to bid and buy anything and everything that took his rabid fancy. Then one day, just as his son was struggling with some success to make his business bloom, Dad made a bid too far.

It happened just when Johnny's fleet of three lorries were working flat out to collect and deliver and fulfil all orders. One day in the midst of this hustle, one lorry and its driver went missing. When it eventually turned up late that evening, the weary driver confessed that Johnny's Dad had told him to go to a far-off farm to pick up a load of junk he had bought in an auction and deliver it to a piece of land in Saffron Waldon.

Johnny's first move was to consult his wise father-in-law on a matter of business ethics and procedure. 'How,' he asked Percy, 'do you fire a shareholder and director of a company?'

'Hmm,' Percy hesitated, having already guessed the cause of the trouble. 'One way would be to cause him to lose his temper so that he would be the one so incensed he would threaten to resign and give up his shares. At that moment you produce the required form already drawn up by your accountant. Hopefully, in his moment of temper, he will sign it.'

The next morning Johnny and his father had the most terrible row, not just about this recent misdemeanour but also a long list of others Johnny dragged up from the past for this special occasion. It certainly had the desired effect. The accusations from son to father were not denied nor apologised for, just immediately and vehemently countered by accusations from father to son. Cries of 'who do you think you are? You can't tell me what to do and what not to do... I can't believe anything you say... You won't listen to anything or anybody...' filled the back kitchen and flowed out into the yard beyond, followed by unforgivable, unforgettable insults hurled back and forth like badminton shuttlecocks between the two shouting opponents. At last came the threatened resignation, though it wasn't put as politely as that.

'If that's how you feel,' said Johnny, hastily producing the necessary document he had handy, 'then all you have to do is sign here'.

'Just give me that pen,' the old man ordered. 'I want no more to do with this company, so it's all yours to run and ruin in any fancy way you feel.' He scrawled an angry signature on the paper and banged out of the house.

So the war was ended, but the peace terms not yet decided. In a day or two of cooling off, Johnny's father Lance, came round to suggest the resignation form be torn up so that hands might be shaken again, but Johnny was adamant. 'Sorry, Dad,' he said, 'but it's too late'. No further explanation. Johnny was pleased to be now in charge of his own destiny, and half of Dad's shares had already been given to Marion.

Now he was in total charge, and with the added responsibility not only of a young wife and a baby son to cater for but also the building and embellishing of a new home in the near future, Johnny thought it might be the time to think about the diversification of his business. The sawdust and chippings business was doing just fine, but there must be some way of adding a bit of gloss.

Sniffing like a bloodhound on the trail for something new and interesting but possible and practicable, Johnny was alerted to the advent of a new company that had opened a factory in Dagenham next door to the Ford motor plant. This new factory was beginning to make chipboard – the very name had a connotation that Johnny could well appreciate – which had originally been made in Russia in the early 1950s. The boards were made from woodchips, dried, re-chipped into splinters and mixed with glue before being squeezed by an enormous press to form sheets or boards. This material, usually measuring eight feet by four and available in various thicknesses became a substitute for plywood and was applicable in a variety of building uses.

Johnny began his introduction to the chipboard world by supplying the factory with woodchips at three pounds a ton. As he became more familiar with the site he noticed a sixteen-foot high pile of chipboards in the manufacturer's yard, covered with plastic sheeting to keep them dry.

Johnny's curiosity sought out the man who might know – and would tell; the weighbridge operator with whom he frequently chatted as his woodchips were weighed in. 'I've seen that stuff over there for several weeks, now,' he said. 'What's it all about, mate?'

'Rejects,' the man replied. 'They're looking for a buyer.'

Johnny immediately realised that here was not only a bargain to be had, but also something that could well serve his long-held philosophy on the subject of shortages.

The time was the middle 60s when the do-it-yourself age was just taking hold, but still without the luxury of the huge super shops where cut-price and buy-one-get-one-free would eventually emerge. Goods such as chipboard were available only to the trade. The DIY man had to dig around, bribe or do without.

These simple facts were, of course, well known to Johnny, but the weighbridge man's information lit up a two hundred and fifty watt light bulb in his head. He made an offer of three pounds ten shillings a ton for the rejects – and that was only ten shillings more than they were paying him for the woodchips. His mental calculator worked out the arithmetic; it looked like the cost to him for each three-quarter-inch chipboard would be only two shillings and nine pence. Not bad.

On the evening of his first acquisition of several tons of chipboard, an advertisement appeared in the Articles for Sale column of the *London Evening News* offering chipboard at ten shillings a sheet – to anybody who bought ten tons. The sale took off immediately and three hundred tons were sold in a few days. As the profit was so good on the deal, Johnny immediately took to paying the factory a thousand pounds in advance to stop any rivals buying the rejects. Now, if any other purchaser came along, Johnny was 'under contract'; no document had been signed, but the firm was happy with his thousand in advance. As time went on this arrangement progressed to a thousand a week. The only other expense in this business was the advertising. The lorries were paid for by the sale of the woodchips. The bank overdraft Johnny had carried since the age of sixteen was ended and the figures on his statement went at last from red to black.

This new diversification from his original theme of farming allied to sawdust was most certainly well within his philosophy of the supply of shortages. He had been aware ever since he left school that England's commercial history led him in that direction. At the age of fourteen, or younger, he had heard that most successful people had earned their livings in the war. So, how was he going to fare unless there was another war? Further investigation showed him that most people had worked for the war and thus had no personal businesses. There had, of course, been some who profited during stringent rationing via the black-market. Of course black-marketeering during war time was considered disgraceful, even criminal, because of the risk to the lives of those who brought the supplies across the waters to our island countries. However, in Johnny's terms, when we won the war, but lost the peace, and rationing was still imposed, some sort of black-marketing was fair game.

Rationing and shortages, Johnny's thoughts continued, involved a mentality people had lived with for many years. In his experience, by Harold Wilson's time as PM, the real shortage was of money. You couldn't borrow to buy a car without fifty percent down. Businesses couldn't borrow unless they were in farming, mining or education. So he started trading heavily on the shortages mentality.

'People bought because they thought something was cheap,' he later admitted, 'when possibly it really wasn't. You see, they were still ration book minded and would buy without too much thought. Housewives would order a Christmas turkey in July, to be sure of getting one.

'For example, when at first I found I could buy reject turkeys from farmers, I could take them into London where the managers of the timber mills would jump at the chance to buy. Sometimes I hadn't even paid for the birds, just exchanged them with a farmer for a load of sawdust!'

Johnny's quick mind then perceived that every type of manufacturer or producer would have substandard goods or end-of-line or shop-soiled display items, all of which could be bought cheaply. Sometimes he sold the goods; sometimes he gave them to a farmer who had bought a large load of sawdust.

'Like this,' he explained... 'Five loads of woodchips purchased in the summer would get you a wardrobe. This gave farm managers who had buying power an incentive to order when they didn't really need to. So I gained a competitive edge over other sawdust merchants.'

Having cracked the method, he expanded it. He decided if he could get meat – beef, pork or lamb – cheaply from the abattoirs he was selling sawdust to, he could earn a lot of money. A company dealing in London, Australia and New Zealand was his first target. He enquired whether they had any meat that they couldn't sell. They replied that everything was sold in advance and nothing ever went wrong. Sorry. However, within a week they phoned him back. A ship in London docks had been unloaded – except for the last ten tons of lamb and as it was Friday afternoon the dockers were refusing to unload the rest. Could Johnny help? Not half!

So he bought ten tons of Number 8 loins for half the London wholesale price. He arranged to deliver the meat to a farmer friend, John Pryor, a former wartime pilot who also, importantly, owned a large walk-in freezer that Johnny knew was empty. It was soon filled with the lamb loins. (Number 8, he had meanwhile learnt, referred to the size of the lamb, which turned out to be very big and very, very fatty.) Johnny invested in a small electric handsaw and sawed each loin into chops and packed them in plastic sacks, each containing about 40 pounds of chops. He knew that freezers were becoming the big food preserving method at the time and he aimed to fill every one in the district. His first move was to pay John Pryor in chops.

The deal didn't turn out as well as he had hoped. The chops were fat and tough and however they were cooked you ended up with a dish of fat. The wife of one of Johnny's friends was away for a month, so Johnny invited him over for dinner at The Chippings each evening. After a couple of weeks he telephoned: 'Thanks, John, it's been great to be with you and Marion. The wine and conversation were fine, but I won't be coming again. I just can't stand another lamb chop!'

Johnny managed to sell about nine tons but as the summer went on the chops deteriorated with freezer-burn, similar to heat burn but caused by the very low temperature of the fridge. The chops became brown, very stringy and now absolutely inedible. The episode ended when not even Johnny could eat his chop for dinner.

He accused Marion. 'I don't think you know how to cook chops,' he said, pushing away his plate.

Marion blew up. 'I have been cooking them twice a day for eighteen months and cooked them every way my recipe books or I could think of. And I even invented a few. It is not my cooking; it's your bloody chops!'

So Johnny sold the last half-ton the next day for dog food and had at least made a profit. He didn't buy meat ever again; he knew he didn't have enough specialist knowledge. While the strategy was good, it was constantly being refined. Today's big business elite would call this 'an emergent strategy'. Johnny didn't know the name for it – but had found it all the same.

Now was the time, Johnny decided, not only to own the house he lived in, but to begin fulfilling his dreams of making it truly the home he and Marion had always wanted. As it stood The Chippings was a red brick bungalow with three bedrooms, a bathroom, toilet, and kitchen. There was also a large lounge, originally intended to embrace a dining room, but, in the building of it, it was decided to have just one very large sitting room. Johnny's first conversion was to install a staircase to lead to a loft This was about to be changed into a large playroom over the whole of the house, using teak veneered chipboard. Of course, this was not the end of Johnny's ideas, but some had to await further finance.

About the time young Mark Anthony John was nearing two years old and answered (occasionally) to the short first one of his names, oddly enough often lengthened to Marco, Marky, or Marcus, his parents decided it was time he had a regular playmate. It didn't matter, they told each other, whether it was a boy or a girl, since it was to be a natural birth like the last, so it was not something they could decide in advance. Nature would take its course and they – and hopefully Mark – would greet the newcomer with happiness and love.

Johnny was not a man to leave things to chance, so this baby's birth was planned as perfectly as the first. But once his job was done and Marion announced she was pregnant, the rest of the proceedings were considered to be 'women's work', so as before Johnny ignored the whole thing and continued with his own job.

Marion decided – much to Johnny's relief – that once the new baby was on its way she would give up teaching dancing and concentrate on looking after her own two children and in any spare time she would take on odd jobs to help her husband's business. There was plenty of time; the baby was not due until the end of February. This time the dreaded morning sickness lasted for only five months, so Marion felt fit and confident enough to tackle anything. During the middle months of her pregnancy Marion began to get her eye in on Johnny's business by answering the phone and taking orders for woodchips and sawdust. One day, however, when an equally pregnant friend, the wife of a cousin who now lived in their old home, Five Oaks, was visiting, a rather more daunting job turned up. Some customers arrived for a load of chipboards and Johnny wasn't about.

'I've never been able to turn a customer away if I could help it, so there was nothing for it but for the two pregnant girls to set to and load up the heavy boards. Neither of us thought it was on the list of recommended exercise for our present state. But we just laughed it off and got on with the job. Apart from being tired and somewhat stiff afterwards, it did us no harm.'

Marion expected the new baby to arrive in the world on time, as Mark had, but this time young Mark almost ruined the family reputation for punctuality. On the last Sunday in January, nearly a month before B-Day, the young mother was busy in her kitchen cooking the lunch. About six members of the family were expected later for tea. Johnny was out and Mark was playing in the sitting room. In that moment everything seemed very normal.

Mark's new toy on that day was a fruit machine that Johnny had bought from an amusement arcade to entertain his young son. It was the type where, for the penny dropped in, several silver balls were released. The flick of a lever would send the balls off to either win or lose. If you won, a packet of sweets dropped out. This particular machine had no key to lock the door from any intruder wishing to investigate its machinery or supply of sweets. The inquisitive young two-year-old was not one to hang about if a short cut could be found, so he opened the door to the huge machine's interior. Suddenly the entire mechanical part of the machine belched out, followed by the whole heavy machine itself, knocking the surprised and terrified child to the floor and pinning him there with his arm trapped under the contraption. His screaming brought his mother swiftly to the rescue. With difficulty she heaved the weighty object away, then picked up the child to cuddle and comfort him.

'Happily there was no real harm done to Mark,' Marion remembered, 'but the lifting and dragging and pushing and pulling at that great thing started my labour a month too soon. Not good.

'That afternoon I could feel things developing, but I said nothing. The family entertainment went ahead as normal and no one noticed. Johnny went to Norfolk the next morning as previously arranged, and I kept my fears to myself, but when I got up the morning after that my waters had broken and the doctor was called in. He agreed I was in labour and said that, hoping to take the baby to full term, I had to stay in bed for the next month. He wanted to stop the waters breaking completely.'

It was now time for Johnny to be sent for, and he came home immediately. He didn't admit it, even to himself, but having previously decided that the baby's birth was not his department, he was now quite worried to find himself involved.

In the early hours of Wednesday, January 31, Marion awoke with what at first she thought were only tummy pains, but the waters broke completely and she was suddenly in strong labour. Johnny telephoned the doctor who told him to go immediately to Ilford Maternity Home and tell them a midwife was urgently required. Of course Marion could not be left alone in labour with a sleeping child in the house, so Johnny sent for her mother, who arrived in a short time accompanied by Marion's sister and grandmother. The old lady knew all there was to know about it, she had been present at several deliveries because, in her day; friends, neighbours and relatives always assisted in such things. As Johnny left for the hospital he instructed father-in-law Percy to stay in his car at the end of the lane in case the midwife passed by without noticing the entrance. Percy didn't know how in the world he was supposed to recognise her. Johnny's organisation hadn't gone that far.

He had his own problems that night, too. He had phoned the hospital for a midwife and arranged to meet her outside Newbury Park station. But he couldn't find her. After a frantic search, he realised he had probably missed her and she was making her own way, so he gave up the search and headed for home.

'I knew the baby was arriving,' said Marion, 'and no nurse, midwife or doctor! As the baby was about to be born, I felt my knickers being snatched off. Everything was happening at the same time. I was in such pain I thought I was going to die. But somehow I didn't. Then when the baby appeared they told me it was another boy. Then they realised they were looking at part of the cord all mixed up, and when they turned the baby over they saw it was a girl. Can you imagine, three grown women looking at a naked little baby and telling the wrong sex! But I suppose they were in a bit of a panic.'

About three-quarters of an hour after the baby had been born, the nurse arrived and also the doctor with his pyjamas still on under his trousers.

The nurse began asking questions and taking notes. When had they first seen the baby's head? Joan replied: 'Ten minutes to three.'

The nurse's next question was: 'What time was the baby born?'

Again Joan's reply was: 'Ten minutes to three.'

The nurse, being very patient, said: 'No dear, you saw the baby's head first…'

'Yes. At ten to three.'

'No, the baby was born, you said at ten to three…'

'Yes.'

'Well, you must have seen the head before that.'

'No.'

'How can that be?'

'Well, she still had her knickers on.'

When Johnny finally arrived home from his fruitless errand he was greeted by the cries of his baby daughter, three exhausted women and the managing midwife who sensibly suggested it would be a good idea for mother and baby to sleep for what was left of the night; that granny and great-granny could be given thanks and sent off home and that the father of the new baby should make himself absent as soon as possible. Everybody was only too happy to oblige

Young Mark, whose desire for sweeties had started the whole dramatic episode, slept peacefully throughout all the night's comings and goings. When he was eventually introduced to his new live-in playmate, he was very happy to meet her. But not so happy about the bossy ladies called 'nurses' who seemed to have taken over the place and who stayed around for about ten days. One day, to try to prevent their entrance, he concocted a trap with a ball of string. He wove the string cunningly back and forth across the front hall from the banisters to the pram, so that when they arrived no one could get across to the door to let them in. First a pair of scissors had to be found to cut a way through Mark's web. As all matters to do with pregnancy, birth or babies were considered by Johnny as woman's work it included giving a name to the little girl who had arrived so dramatically and prematurely. So when Marion had recovered her own strength after the turbulent happenings of the previous days, she gave some calming and pleasing thoughts to the job.

'I chose our children's names,' she said. 'Johnny would never come up with any suggestions or even discuss the matter. Jennie was a name I thought both pretty and practical. We were also friendly with a girl who went on to become an actress. Her name was Belinda Sinclair. She was the daughter of an actress and singer called Nicolette Roeg. So our little girl was named Jennie Belinda.

'Some years later when Jennie was about eight there was a TV show starring Hywell Bennet and Belinda Sinclair, so I'm happy to say that Jennie got to see the girl she was named after.'

The young father was only too happy to leave these maternal duties to Marion who he considered very capable in that department, especially now she had decided to give up running the dancing schools she shared with her sister Joyce. For some mysterious masculine reason he had always resented the time she spent away from home – and him – doing a job he considered useless. He was relieved that the decision was hers, not his, to give her first thoughts to her own children and family.

Now that the home front was completely adequately guarded and cared for, he could concentrate more fully on the manly task of being the provider of all the good things of life. And, as ever, that had to start with cash in bank and pocket.

Every man who becomes successful in his business has found somewhere along the line the prod or spur to motivate him devotedly and single-mindedly towards the star leading him to his own private promised land. The stimulus in Johnny's case had come, in a way, from his father, Lance, but curiously in a negative rather than positive way.

'My old man was an auction-aholic,' Johnny explains. 'He couldn't resist bidding for anything, everything he fancied –mostly junk. Rusty old mowers. Bits of bikes. Old books. He went to Chelmsford cattle market every week where they had a rubbish market alongside the cattle. He spent all the family's spare money buying useless stuff. When I was a kid living at home I had seen all the money trickle out and I guess it frightened me so much I have had this fear of going skint ever since.'

In every man's life there are no doubt reasons for not wanting to become bankrupt, or 'skint' as Johnny calls it. But in his life it is possible there were more than most. Well, if not more reasons, certainly different ones. He couldn't, no he *couldn't* let himself down that way in front of Marion's parents. Her father, Percy, was his idol, mentor, example and friend. Her mother, Joan, had never quite accepted him as the Prince Charming she had visualised for her daughter. Johnny was secretly certain that if the dreaded skint-situation ever arrived there would be an 'I-told-you-so' halo over the head of his mother-in-law.

Being seen as bankrupt by the neighbours (those were his in-laws) was bad enough, but being known as skint by the farmers who were his customers and friends, was something else again – and possibly even worse. Johnny had always been a courageous, even daring, chap except for this dark dread that occasionally overtook him. He thought about it, feared it, even talked about it to anyone who would listen. Seeking what? Sympathy? Laughter? Help? Dismissal? Diagnosis? Kindred spirits? No, none of that. Perhaps it was merely an acknowledgement to his secret self and to anyone smart enough to see, that the fear was actually the goad that prodded him on to achieve the successes he desired.

Sadly there seemed no happy ending to Johnny's dilemma, for the more successful he became the greater grew the fear bedevilling him, because he well knew that the higher you went the further you had to fall. Also, the more you would lose in the way of comforts, good housing, holidays, luxuries – large or small. Like losing a throw of dice in a board game, you would have to go back to the beginning. And he could remember what that was like.

Marion, with her practical feminine mind, had no such fear. And was rather dismissive when he brought the subject up. 'I found it a bit odd,' she admitted. 'Surely he can see his state of affairs, his bank balance, the money still owed to him, that sort of thing. So he must know that unless something extreme happens, going skint is unlikely. Anyway, all businesses run this risk, so what's it all about?

'And so I said to him that if it was all too much worry for him he should just give it all up and go and get a nine to five job for a regular wage.'

Johnny quoted Marion's wisdom to several people over the years, while still stressing his fears. Then at some time he decided she was probably right, especially about the same risk run by all businesses and his fears seemed to calm down.

'He still talks about going skint sometimes, though,' Marion added. 'I think it might now be a sort of party piece. Maybe I'm wrong, but I don't think so.'

During 1968 the Good Fairy (or whatever) had waved a wand and granted two wishes to the Inkster family. The first had been the safe birth to Marion of their lovely little daughter, Jennie. The second didn't take nine months, but to Johnny it seemed longer. He could now admit even to himself that he was enjoying his successes in his work, but now a new problem niggled at the back of his mind. He resolved that something must be done about it.

Chapter Five
Symbols of Success

Johnny's problem loomed larger and larger the more he thought about it. The trouble was that he knew he was making a success of his life and business. A wife and two children, a new home and some money in the bank. But…

But nobody else seemed to notice his advancing status. He was aware that friends, relatives and even customers still saw him as the hard-working young man who earned a bob or two sweeping up sawdust in London's East End; or as the pleasant, talkative chap who delivered wood-chips to the farms of Essex. What he felt he needed, was something that would show them. A symbol, a token that all could observe, admire, envy; something that would prove to friends, neighbours, family and customers his increasing importance and social circumstance. But what? He could hardly hang his bank statement from his lapel for all to see and his was not the kind of business that would provide him with a gong, a medal or an honour from the Queen. Somewhere there was the right outward and visible sign – but where?

Then one day, out of the blue, there it was. An advertisement tucked away in the crowded columns of small ads in the magazine *Exchange and Mart,* required reading at that time by all traders and bargain hunters. The ad offered for sale, with box number for application, a Rolls Royce for £3,500.

Johnny sent off an immediate letter making an offer of £3,000 and waited impatiently for a reply. 'They're waiting for someone to up the ante,' he told himself during the brief delay, but he was not going to be that someone... yet.

Then one day it came, no mention of acceptance, or otherwise, of the offer, but a suggestion that he should come up to Liverpool to see the car. Liverpool was a world away from Johnny's sphere of knowledge. However, the next morning he went to the bank and drew out the three thousand pounds in cash and took the notes home immediately.

'You are not to leave the house as long as this money is here,' he ordered Marion. 'And don't think you can hide it anywhere and dash out to the shops. Burglars know every hiding place you can think of. Even if you have a safe they can get into it. We'll never have a safe. It's just a signal that you've got something good enough to hide.'

During that day Marion had every intention of obeying Johnny's orders until the baby started crying and she discovered the milk bottle was empty. She tried everything she knew to quieten the child, rocking her, offering her toys, even trying to attract the little one's attention to something else, but the tiny eyes remained tight shut, squeezing out the tears and gradually the baby's face grew red with frustrated anger.

'Well,' Marion told herself, 'there's more than one way of killing a cat or of shushing a baby.' And she took up the wads of notes and spread them all over the bottom of the pram, covered them with the waterproof sheet, then added a blanket, the pillow and the baby whose cries had subsided somewhat as she wondered what was going on. Marion locked the door behind her and wheeled the pram with its doubly precious cargo off to the local shop to buy a bottle of milk.

But Marion had reckoned without her husband's impatience and the trip to the shop took longer than she expected. By the time she got home, Johnny was already there, tearing the place apart looking for his money. She had hardly got the pram and Mark through the front door before he was shouting: 'Where is it? Have you hidden it, or has it been nicked? I told you not to leave the house when the money was here. I TOLD YOU…'

Calmly, quietly but quickly, before Johnny had turned their home into a jumble sale, Marion removed Jennie and the waterproof sheet from the pram to reveal the scattered notes. While Johnny collected up his money and began counting it, Marion warmed up some milk for their daughter. Soon there was a sweet silence. No crying, no shouting.

Early the next morning Johnny and his friend Peter Hyland divided up the £3000 into two bundles of £1,500; each man tucking his own portion safely away into an inner pocket. Then they set out for Euston Station to catch an early train to Lime Street, Liverpool. On arrival there they were met by the company's accountant with the Rolls Royce parked nearby.

Johnny held his breath and stifled a triumphant grin at his friend as they climbed aboard the glittering car to give it a test drive round Liverpool's city centre. 'I've just got to have it,' Johnny told himself, 'well, it's a Mark III and my pa-law Percy's is only a Mark I!' While Johnny, experiencing alternating waves of anxiety and excitement, guided the purring vehicle through the busy traffic of this strange city, Peter made a note of all the dashboard gadgets and even took a peep into the glove box. After about half an hour's run the accountant, seated in the back, guided them to the Maiden office where Johnny and Peter reluctantly left the Rolls and accompanied him to the office he shared with the son of Arthur Maiden, the firm's founder.

Johnny didn't stand on ceremony or beat about the bush. 'I'll have it,' he told the two surprised businessmen, 'and here's the money.' And he laid out his half of the notes and signalled Peter to do the same.

The accountant didn't touch the notes, but frowned and shook his head. 'Oh, no,' he announced sternly. 'We can't accept cash.' Maiden's son nodded agreement.

At that Johnny's anger and voice rose. 'What? I've never heard a refusal for cash, before. Not ever!' He banged his fist loudly on the table and his voice filled the small room. 'Are you making out we nicked it? Because if you are...' But before he could issue whatever threat he had in mind, one of the office doors was flung open by an angry elderly gentleman.

'What is going on in here? What is all the shouting about?'

The accountant stood up – almost to attention – and began an explanation. 'Ah, Mr Maiden. So sorry if you've been disturbed. These – er – young men want to buy your old Rolls Royce – for cash – *cash!*'

Before the newcomer could make any comment or reply, Peter Hyland stood up and rushed across the room towards him. 'Mr Arthur Maiden?' he queried, taking him by his hand to shake. 'Oh, I have always wanted to meet you, the owner of that magnificent racehorse, Ballet Russ.'

Johnny's anger subsided into amazement. He had no idea, and found it difficult to believe, that his friend knew anything at all about racehorses. But the surprises were not yet ended.

The old man clapped Peter on the shoulder with the hand that was not being vigorously shaken and said, smiling: 'You must both come into my office and see some pictures of Ballet Russ and some of my other horses,' and quickly led the way back through the door he had just stormed through.

The meeting of this trio could not have gone better. Luckily for the two likely lads, Mr Maiden, proudly bragging about his string of racehorses, did most of the talking. Johnny did try one daring question, hesitantly, because he was not at all sure of his facts.

'You're in the advertising business, aren't you, Mr Maiden?'

'Well,' Arthur Maiden replied, 'I am if you count bill-posting on large hoardings all over the country as advertising.'

Both the young men nodded. Of course they had often seen the name labelled on the foot of many a huge road or rail-side poster. Arthur Maiden was the founder of the successful and growing Liverpool firm.

For half an hour or more the elderly gentleman entertained his guests with stories of his racing days, showing them pictures of the favourite nags. Then, as it appeared the flattery of their attention had appealed to him, he announced that of course he would accept their cash for his car, and immediately opened the communicating door to the accountant's office. To .the two men working there he ordered; 'Give the keys of my old car to Mr Inkster. Of course I will accept his cash offer – after all, he probably won it on one of my horses!' he laughed, then turned to Johnny. 'Take the whole thing as it is – in pretty good nick. But you can't have the registration number, AM10. OK?'

'Of course, Mr Maiden,' Johnny agreed and promised to proceed with re-registration as soon as he reached home.

Johnny and Peter eagerly grasped the keys, and with handshakes and thanks all round departed to pick up the splendid car awaiting them. As they were giving it a good once-over, Johnny asked Peter the question that had been bothering him during the past hour.

'How did you know about the old man's racehorse and its name?'

With a sly wink and a proud thumb-behind-his-lapel gesture Peter replied: 'Easy, mate,' and as he spoke opened the glove box in front of his passenger seat and took out a photograph of a handsome racehorse. On the back of the picture was the name of the horse; Ballet Russ, and a caption to the effect that it was owned by Mr Arthur Maiden of Liverpool.

'You cunning bugger,' announced Johnny as he started up the purring engine to begin the 200 miles or so journey back to Essex.

Johnny was very chuffed with his new car, and immediately bought himself a Stetson to wear while at the wheel, obviously fancying himself as a Texan oil millionaire. In Essex? Well, he could dream, couldn't he? He was also particularly pleased that father-in-law's Rolls was only a Mark 1, and maroon, while his was Mark III and dressed in sleek, shiny black. He already knew he had 'arrived' – now, wrapped at last in this obvious symbol of his success, all the witnessing world would recognise it.

Early on in his acquisition he decided to use the car as a business tool, after all it was the people he met during his working life – which was nearly all of it – who he hoped would nod their heads in approval, blink an eye in awe, or quietly agree that 'they always knew he had it in him'. So the Rolls Royce and the Stetson accompanied him to collect debts or orders from his farmer friends and occasionally took him to London's East End to check that his fleet of lorries were doing the job they had been bought for.

'I don't care if I don't earn another penny,' he confessed, 'as long as I stay out of the red. And I like acting like I own a million, that's why I drive the Rolls in a Stetson. But, it'll only ever be an act.'

The kind of business Johnny ran neither desired nor required nor ever acquired an office. Johnny himself did not take to the idea of being desk bound, surrounded by such personnel as secretaries, accountants and the like. His was very much the one-man band. He was the sole mover and shaker. He recognised, however, that even in that unilateral style of working there had to be some communication with the rest of the world, so he invented the Coffee Rounds. It is extremely unlikely that young Inkster was aware of the importance of the coffee houses to education, commerce and the arts during London's booming Restoration years. It would never have occurred to Johnny that the original denizens such as Dr Samuel Johnson, the diarist Pepys and many Fleet Street figures of the late 1600s conducted their businesses in much the same way by the collection and delivery of news by word of mouth. He would not have known when he introduced the Coffee Rounds to his confreres in the world of sawdust, timber and farming, that he was echoing the origins of the world famous insurance firm Lloyds of London, the birthplace of which was the coffee house of one Edward Lloyd whose customers came to discuss shipping and ships as they sipped the dark brown brew made from beans transported from across the seas

However, even if Johnny Inkster, farmer, wood merchant, trader – however he styled himself then – had been aware of the renaissance coffee houses, he would have thought it a great idea and adopted it immediately.

The conversations in the Inkster Coffee Rounds were of the 'shoes and ships and sealing wax and cabbages and kings' variety. In fact anything that came to mind was a valid topic. Johnny's original *raison d'etre* for the meetings was to collect monies owing from the farmers, and to take new orders, but the gossip and the intrigue and the standard of local culture became so fascinating that it mattered not what subjects came to the fore. It was all a kind of further education for the young man who was eager to know anything about everything.

At that time Johnny's working days began early, Marion would prod him awake with an ancient shepherd's crook she kept handy for the job, and soon after breakfast he would drive off in the Rolls Royce to his first coffee rendezvous where he hoped to pick up an order or two for woodchips or sawdust.

He was a raconteur *par excellence* who could keep an audience silent and enthralled until it burst into a hurricane of laughter or a shout of amazed gasps. And there was teasing aplenty among the Coffee Rounders. There was, for example, the tale of Oxygen Lewis.

Johnny's Rolls usually rolled up for his first cuppa at Bob Garratt's immaculate riding school around ten-thirty in the morning. As a young man Bob had been in the Horse Guards and had ridden just behind the Queen's coach at the time of her coronation. Ever since his demobilisation he had owned a riding school in Aldborough Hatch, Essex, which he ran with military precision and the adults and children he taught benefited from the guardsman's discipline.

One day Bob greeted Johnny's arrival with the shocking news that one of their coffee companions, Dick Lewis, had been 'nicked by the coppers' for – of all things – thieving.

A most unlikely event, thought Johnny; after all, Dick and his wife Mary were staunch pillars of the local scene, regular churchgoers and the least likely of anyone they knew to have stolen anything. No, there must be some mistake.

But it transpired that the sad – and true – tale went something like this:

It seemed that Dick's combine harvester frequently became clogged up with the dust and dirt it had travelled through in its work. Dick tried spraying out the dirt with water, but the only result of that was that the combine then became clogged worse with mud. A passing lorry driver, whose vehicle, belonging to the British Oxygen Company, was stored in Dick's farmyard, saw the farmer's problem.

'Hey, Dick,' he called out, 'what you want for that job is oxygen to blow out the mud'. He took a cylinder of the stuff from his lorry, and demonstrated for the farmer. All the dust, mud and dirt vanished before you could say BOC. Grateful for Dick's co-operation in allowing him free shelter for his vehicle, he said he would leave the odd cylinder on occasion for Dick to use as and when he desired.

All went well until BOC discovered there was a cylinder missing from their stock. Eventually, it was traced to the lorry driver who, in all innocence, advised them where it could be found. A young police inspector was sent to investigate and discovering the whereabouts of the missing item, asked no questions but arrested the farmer, and took him off to the cells for the night. Next morning he was charged with theft.

That was the story so far and as Bob paused for breath and to take a swig of coffee, in walked a very worried Dick Lewis.

'Morning, mates,' he mumbled as he poured out a mug of the mahogany liquid. 'What do you think I ought to do now? Is there any way out, or am I going into the nick for God knows how long?'

Johnny, deep in thought, brightened when he heard that Dick was to appear before the magistrates. 'There's no problem, Dick. Here's what you must do...' and he outlined the ploy.

'You must opt to go for trial by jury and make sure you reserve your defence...'

Dick interrupted him to say he was so worried about the whole affair, he feared he might say the wrong thing in court.

'No problem,' was Johnny's immediate response. He was, after all, the son of a policeman and therefore was familiar with the system and knew the procedure. He wrote out all that was likely to happen and everything that Dick should say and do.

Dick nervously but gratefully read Johnny's brief, took the advice and eventually went for trial where the jury found him Not Guilty.

Later a celebratory supper was held in the Dick Turpin pub opposite the church where Dick Lewis was a warden; even the vicar came to give his support. It was decided, by Johnny, that Dick should pay for all the food and wine that night. 'It's the usual practice,' he teased, 'for East End villains who have got off.' That evening Dick became known as 'Oxygen Lewis' and the name stuck for ever more.

A week or so later, Johnny found a notice nailed to his back door, it announced: 'John Inkster – Barrister at Law'. It was Oxygen Lewis's way of saying Thanks.

Johnny was at last content that the rest of his world had recognised that his place in it was now at least one step up. But, he decided there were still things to do to add to his value. His home, for example, was his office (insofar as he had one) and also a family dwelling. He was aware that his business as well as his children were growing, so more space would soon have to be found for all of it.

Up to now the house had belonged to Percy, rented from him at three pounds fifty a week, but Johnny's urge to be independent made him hungry to own his own home, so he could set about to make the alterations he and Marion dreamed of. But, first, he told himself, the old adage about all work and no play was very true and as he found he had about a thousand pounds surplus to requirements – not enough to buy the house and start that work but he decided he would use it first to deal with another dream.

Many Englishmen, it seems, have a hankering for the sea, some to become sailors or fishermen or lifeboat men; others, more desk or work-habit bound, crave for an ocean cruise or to own a yacht of their own. To many the desire of the off-shore views, or the lust for the beauty, excitement, sometimes hypnotic fear of the waves combine with wanderlust and a secret hope of being out of sight and out of touch with the humdrum daily grind.

It was like that for Johnny and the dream had come unasked, unsought in those carefree pre- and early marriage days when he accompanied Percy and the Beaumont family to holidays in Torquay. There, he and the man who eventually became his father-in-law left the women to their shopping and baby-care and tore around the bay in a speedboat called *Cider* – not only was it the fastest craft in the area but it had a royal connection. Princess Margaret, it was said, had learnt to water-ski behind it.

Now that thousand pounds was itching to be spent on a boat of his own and Johnny found one for the right price in his favourite periodical *Exchange and Mart*. It was for sale in the fens on an inland waterway near Cambridge. Percy, however, sniffed when Johnny showed him the picture in the advertisement. 'It's got Venetian blinds,' he sneered, 'You can't have a boat with Venetian blinds – it wouldn't be seamanlike.'

Stimulated by the mention of boats, Percy pointed to another advertisement along the page. A 40ft veteran of

Dunkirk was for sale at the snip price of £3,000. It was on the Thames at Eton.

'Yeah, great,' agreed Johnny. 'But I haven't got three thou.'

'Well,' said the older man. 'I'd be willing to come in with you on the deal. Anyway, let's go and see it.'

The two boat lovers took the next day off and travelled to Eton in Johnny's Rolls, but parked the car well out of sight when they neared the location. 'Don't want to give 'em the idea of shoving the price up,' Johnny muttered.

Percy immediately fell in love with the boat. It reminded him of similar ones cruising past Southend pier in his youth, and Johnny was quite contented to put up his thousand pounds and borrowed the other five hundred pounds for his half from Percy. It took him a month or two to pay it back.

The old boat, called *Iorana*, meaning Tahitian Flower, stayed on the Thames and served both families well for a year or so, in fact until Johnny needed to finance the purchase of his home. He had managed to save two thousand five hundred and borrowed ten thousand on short term loan from Barclays Bank. His half share of the boat would just raise the required sum up to the fourteen thousand pounds Percy was asking for the house. A deal was struck and in the end Percy owned the boat, but Johnny owned the house.

His first improvement to his purchase was for the sake of business rather than family. A large agricultural barn was built in the grounds to store woodchips and to service his growing fleet of lorries, now all smartly painted in bright yellow with red signwriting. All present profits were going into the purchase of new lorries and to expansion in his company by supplying more and larger farms.

The next move on the home front was to please Marion. A large kitchen extension was added to the back of the house. There Marion employed an architect to design the interior complete with an Aga; a huge American six-foot fridge; a waste disposal unit; a cool top hob that cooked with magnetism plus a separate service annex which housed a washing machine, ironing board, and dishwasher. It also included a shower room for Johnny to clean up in when he arrived home covered in sawdust and woodchips.

On Friday evenings the lorry drivers would all come into the kitchen for coffee and to collect their wages and chat over the week's work. The dining area of the kitchen where they met was furnished with a huge table, specially built to be more than an arm's length wide, so that the drivers couldn't punch each other across the table when they discussed who earned how much that week.

The toddler, Mark, played around the drivers' feet and from the age of three was allowed to 'drive' the lorries up and down the lane by sitting on the drivers' laps and steering the vehicles. As the drivers all addressed his father as Johnny, the young Mark came to do so also. 'Dad' became a term used only on birthday cards and letters and even then only occasionally.

The next move to add another touch of luxury for the family was an indoor swimming pool attached to the house. During the construction of this Johnny ruled that nobody was allowed in the back garden. He feared somebody would fall into the vast hole being dug there. One night when going up the yard he took a short cut across the hole on a scaffold plank which sprung up and catapulted him into the muddy bottom of the pool. He was lucky not to be badly hurt and also that his shower room was close at hand.

When the pool house was eventually finished three more bedrooms were built above it and soon afterwards another extension was added for a second living room and office.

By the time the work on the house, called The Chippings, was finished and most of the bills paid and the money borrowed from the bank repaid – it all took about eighteen months – Johnny's hunger for a boat of his own returned. Marion, unlike many wives of boat-loving husbands, liked the water herself and joined with Johnny in the purchase of a twin-engined sports boat called a Cleopatra. It was twenty-three feet in length and flew over the water. They kept it at Wallasey Island in Essex for a couple of years, then took it up the Thames to meet up with Percy and *Iorana*.

One rainy day, Johnny sat on board his boat dreaming of his next business move while reading *Motorboat and Yachting*. There he spotted an advertisement for a Grand Banks, which told of the comforts of this large vessel complete with an upper deck called a flying bridge. He and Marion took a day off for a demonstration – that's all it was to be – and the salesman took them on a trip across the Solent to Cowes. Before they reached Calshot they had bought this super American motor yacht for £9,250. Only £6,450 to Johnny, for he sold the Cleopatra for £2,800. The Grand Banks was wonderful; it felt like owning a ship.

Of course, a boat of that size needed a mooring – the elegant sort with a harbourmaster, a car park, water and electricity laid on. Where better than one of the Hamble river marinas which had all those things and was also handy for exploring Southampton Water to see the big liners and ferries making their way to dock, a safe and interesting refuge on days when the Solent forecast offered only high winds against spring tides making rough, uncomfortable journeys.

A month or so after the acquisition of the Grand Banks and its mooring, Johnny's accountant visited to audit the firm's accounts. With a little hesitation, the accountant friend confessed: 'I'm sorry John,' but I can't clear these accounts for you.'

Johnny frowned, this was unusual. 'Why not?'

'Well,' the accountant explained, 'there's a fairly large sum that I can't fathom. It's just disappeared.'

'How much?' Johnny asked.

'Six thousand, four hundred and fifty pounds. It's just gone.'

'Oh, I know where that is,' said Johnny, and he gave a little chuckle.

'Where?'

'Sailing down the Hamble river…'

Marion loved the new boat as much as Johnny, but as it was their first craft on open water and the children were only two and four years old and neither she nor her husband were swimmers, she decided to take charge.

'I couldn't put my confidence and the children's safety, on any one else's shoulders but my own,' she said. 'So I went with my father to navigation and sailing lessons. We did capsize drill and all the usual and finally got our yachting certificates.

'Which was just as well because one day as we left Weymouth to return to the Hamble, the weather broke and became heavy. The sea was rough and we tossed and rolled. Johnny and Jennie were both seasick and lying down, so there was nothing for it but to take the boat back myself. Mark came and sat beside me. It was company during a nervous time.

'I did the whole of the journey and was pleased at last to see the Needles through the spray. In the Solent the water was calmer and I was thinking that when I reached the Hamble river I would radio the harbourmaster and ask someone to come on board and berth the boat for me. I had never done it before and it's very tricky when there's a strong tide and wind blowing – and we had both!

'Fortunately, the calmer Solent waters cured Johnny enough for him to take the boat in himself as usual. But I was quite chuffed at my own performance that day.'

In the meantime, when on shore Johnny quelled any financial worries by spending a little time improving his mind and skills with a programme of education. Like everything else in John Inkster's philosophy, it was unconventional, to say the least. The 'college' he joined was as a member of the Processed Sawdust, Woodchip Association. His 'tutors' were the other members, all older and more experienced than he in the same trades. The meetings took place every six weeks and began at eleven a.m. in the well stocked bar of the Terenure Club where most of the members braced themselves with a drink or two in the hour until lunch was served.

'I didn't drink in those days,' said Johnny. 'I was just there to listen and learn more about the business from these older men who had dealt in sawdust and woodchips for many years and had learnt a lot of tricks of the trade along the way.

'Well, that first luncheon was an eye-opener to me, I'd never been out to a lunch before. And this was really posh, several courses and drinks. It was always held in the same place, a posh part of Barnet, North London, among posh houses. Oh, it was great.

'The first course was always lobster or smoked salmon – a rarer treat in those days than now. After that came a choice of a huge T-bone steak or Dover sole the size of a door mat. Then the meal ended up with mountains of strawberries.

'It was wonderful; taught me a lot. I even brushed up on new jokes before the next meeting to entertain the other members – one of whom was a local bigwig, an earnest Tory and big fan of Mrs. Thatcher. So with his influence the talk was often on politics – accompanied by much drinking and shouting. It was my introduction to boozy lunches where money was no object. That lunch cost between twenty-six and twenty-eight pounds a head – a small fortune in those days. But, blimey, it was worth it.'

The actual official meeting of the Processed Sawdust, Woodchip Association began immediately after the luncheon's final brandy and coffee session. The meetings were conducted by a very efficient professional company secretary hired from the London Chamber of Commerce. There were all the proper motions: apologies from absentees; minutes of the last meeting and an agenda dealing with such important kindred subjects as The State of Trade; any new laws affecting the conduct of the trades; traffic and trucking problems; weights and measures and any other business. There were drinks served throughout; this did not help to speed the proceedings which usually ran until about four in the afternoon.

By the time they reached any other business, all hell let loose, Johnny remembers. The wine and spirits were firing the dealers. They were all yelling at each other: 'You've sneaked into my factory – spying and stealing'… 'Rubbish! Who knows more about stealing than you – my sacks don't just fly out of the window'… 'You're all undercutting me. It's got to be stopped. There should be a law…'

'The poor guy, the secretary, tried to regain his hold on affairs by shouting them down that this was not a cartel. These arguments couldn't be minuted, and so on. But nothing stopped the drunken arguments.'

Marion, a ready, willing and amused audience for the tales of these Terenure club meetings detailed for her on every occasion when Johnny came home, referred to them as 'The Woodchopper's Ball', and promised young Mark that when he was sixteen he could go along, too.

What with the cost of the Terenure lunches, of the building at home and of the money floating down the Hamble river, there seemed to be a lot of cash seeping out of Johnny's bank account just then. 'Having a boat,' someone told him, 'is like making a hole in the water to pour money into'. What with the mooring fees at the Hamble marina; repairs and repainting; hauling the boat out of the water every spring to see there was no wear and tear under the waterline and having the bottom anti-fouled and all the little extras, that chap was quite right, Johnny admitted to himself. However the business was doing all right, so there was nothing really to worry about. 'But,' as he knew, 'you never know what's waiting around the next corner'.

Bernard Matthews, the well-known huge turkey farmer, was a good customer for wood chips and sawdust and Johnny's lorries visited regularly with numerous sacks of the firm's produce until one day when his lorry driver came back from the Matthews farm with a curious – and very disturbing – story.

'They didn't want our sacks of chips,' the driver said, indicating his still-full lorry. 'And it doesn't look like they'll ever want any more.'

Johnny felt his heart miss a beat as the man continued. 'Y'see, they've got a new product now. It's a sort of plastic bale, with a lot more woodchips in the bale than a same size sack would hold, because they're condensed during baling. I spotted some being delivered and each bale is about three-foot by two-foot, and so just dandy for stacking into the lorries. Cor, Johnny, you ought to have seen 'em. Nothin' like I've ever seen before.'

As the man's voice trailed off in wonder, Johnny felt the sweat of fear rise to his brow. 'It looked like the beginning of the end of my business,' Johnny confessed later. 'And that old dread of going skint rose up again and choked in my throat. It didn't need any further descriptions from the lorry driver to show me how dangerous this new product was for me. Sacks to carry our wares had never been a great idea – but what else? They wore out quickly, were not very hygienic. Some of the big farmers, like Bernard Matthews, were always cautious if sacks looked old; they were afraid they might carry germs dangerous to their poultry – like foul pest. So this new invention, wherever it came from, was obviously an ideal answer, plus plastic covered to keep the woodchips dry even if stored outside. Oh, I could see it all.

'I tried to comfort myself with the knowledge I could still undersell them. The new bales were eight shillings each; I charged two bob for a sack and one bale was approximately equal to three sacks. But it was a small hope for a short time until the other farmers got wind of the plastic bales. I could see the writing on the wall – and it spelled SKINT.'

Although downhearted, Johnny was not yet beaten. He was determined to find out as much as he could about this new process and then decide what the knowledge would tell him.

Chapter Six
Going Dutch

Johnny was not the sort of man to be depressed for long, or at any rate to admit it even to himself. Especially when there was a project in view. The present project was one of discovery, a bit of detective work here and there. It was essential to his own livelihood to find out all he could about this dangerous, but admittedly devilishly clever, innovation that he feared could eventually ruin him. And how long was 'eventually'? That was the big question that stirred his head to wakefulness during a sleepless night. How long had he got before all his customers, loyal or not-so-loyal (after all, they had to look after Number One, too) said, 'Sorry, Johnny, we don't want those old sacks any more. We've taken up with the new plastic covered bales'. Not even his boozy friends at his Terenure Club could help him now and, anyway, he didn't want them to get wind of the new process before he had sussed it all out himself. No, he was a man on his own. Neither could Marion's wise words help him now, nor even Percy's worldly knowledge. His coffee mates would also have to find these things out later – much later – for themselves. It was better to keep his own worries to himself, and see what a little 'spying' could do.

Johnny always had a bit of luck to start him off, this time it was seasonal. The summer was always the most difficult period to sell sawdust and woodchips to farmers because their cows, pigs and horses were kept outdoors as much as possible, sleeping in the fields and cropping the good grass instead of the expensive cattle cake and other winter fodder. It was a money-saving time for their owners. This momentary lack of trade gave Johnny time to explore his problem and gather any pertinent gossip from the coffee rounds.

It was a Dutch company, he heard, who were baling woodchips all over Europe – Holland, Germany, Belgium, Switzerland, France, and now England. It seemed they had a baling machine designed and built by themselves and were currently handling more than three thousand tons of material a week. Johnny's first contact with the actual baling machine was when one was set up in a timber mill in King's Lynne.

But it was only via a casual glance as he passed by when picking up a small load of chippings for his own firm. The mill didn't want to part with as many as usual as they needed all of their supply to feed their own baling machine.

Then came his next piece of luck. He heard that Phoenix Timber Ltd, a large sawmill operating on the banks of the river Thames in Rainham, Essex, had acquired a baling machine from the Dutch company. Phoenix was about fifteen minutes from home, near enough to drive over to see what he could see and sniff out any possible business for himself.

On that quick look around, Johnny picked up two useful clues. He learnt that Phoenix mills were not producing enough of the raw material (soft woodchips) required to keep the baling machine fully busy. His inquisitive eyes also fell upon a huge pile of the bales stacked outside in the yard. Were they rejects, he wondered. If so, perhaps he could repeat the performance he had found so lucrative in the chipboard business. Buying cheap and selling off at a bargain price, was in his veins.

During his boating days that weekend, Johnny had plenty to occupy his mind. On his spying trip to Phoenix he had learnt that the Dutch company had formed a separate company for their local work. It was called General Chip Co, and was being run by the original two Dutch brothers and an English general manager called Gerald Hart. What Johnny needed now was an entry into that manager's office.

By one of those happy coincidences that seemed to happen in Johnny's life, one of his more interesting boating mates came alongside that weekend. He was in the insurance business, but looked more like a poet with his goatee beard. He was always smartly dressed in the blazer he wore in honour of his boating days. His name was Les Hancock and the two weekend boaters always enjoyed a chat over a drink on one boat or the other.

'That weekend,' Johnny remembered, 'the subject was his line of work. I wanted to pick his brain. You see he was an insurance inspector, especially in the commercial sector. He travelled around inspecting this place and that to make sure the companies he visited were properly covered for fire or flood or whatever.

'So, I happened to mention the thing that was on my mind at the time. It was a casual enquiry at first, I just asked him what was the position of – say – large stores of waste, such as several hundred tons of baled up woodchips lying around in piles outside a timber mill?

'He was a pretty smart chap, pricked up his ears right off and flung out the right question: Did I know of such a thing, and if so, where? Well, I did. I told him about all those piles of bales parked in the yard of the Phoenix mill.' Johnny didn't realise it then, but he couldn't have picked a more useful person to discuss his problem with than this unlikely boating pal.

'Of course I didn't know it, but you see Phoenix happened to be one of the companies his firm did business with. He said he'd be off to see them straight away, and left his boat that evening.'

Early Monday morning Les Hancock, primed with Johnny's information, visited the wood mill, inspected the huge pile of bales stored near buildings and declared it an obvious fire hazard. He lost no time in seeing the manager and told him firmly that the bales had to be moved immediately, or he would cause the baling company to be shut down. Within twenty-four hours there was a board meeting, the outcome of which was that Hancock was asked to advise if he knew anyone who could get rid of the stuff quickly for them.

'Well,' he said, 'there's a very big man in the wood business. I've often seen his fleet of lorries around this area. Maybe he could help.'

Johnny answered the urgent phone call immediately and set out in his black Rolls Royce, parking it as near to the Phoenix Timber managing director's office as he could get. Just as he was locking it up to leave, a couple of men with buckets and wash leathers came by and asked if they should wash the car. Pretty good service, this, thought Johnny, as he nodded his agreement. He learnt later that the Phoenix managing director also had a black Rolls, which he parked in the same place... However, nobody said anything and John's car had a good free wash and polish.

A girl in the reception told him he was expected, and asked him to go straight up to see Mr Victor Serry in the MD's office on the top floor.

'Two important chaps were there – Serry of Phoenix and Gerald Hart of the Dutch baling machine General Chip Company. There was no ceremony as I entered,' Johnny remembered. 'I just said who I was, and the MD's reply

99

straight off was to ask if I could get rid of two thousand tons of bales. 'Yes,' I said.

'How soon?' he asked.

'Immediately, if that's what you want,' I told them. Immediate was the key word. There were eight tons to the lorry load, so I knew I would have to hire more transport, but I agreed it could be done.

'And it would be done – on condition. The condition was that I could buy the bales I was removing at two shillings and sixpence each – with a contract for this lot and any further rejects. The MD agreed – he hadn't got a lot of choice. And the contract included buying further rejects at the same price.'

So, the deed was done to the satisfaction of one and all – especially Johnny, who sold the bales he had bought at two and six for eight shillings each to his friendly farmers who were delighted to have bales they could store, even outdoors, until required – much better than the smelly old sacks that took up valuable indoor accommodation in stables or barns.

And now he had formed a friendly relationship with Gerald Hart, Johnny was determined to press home his advantage. As he had already found on his earlier voyage of discovery, the Phoenix Mill produced only about sixty to eighty tons a week of the desired woodchips to keep the baling machine active. Hart was having to buy extra shavings from smaller mills in East London and the Home Counties. Which would cost him – plus transport. As it was the summertime lull in his own trade with farmers, Johnny offered to supply woodchips at two pounds a ton, knowing full well that the bales should be filled with ninety-five percent of the first quality material (soft woodchips and sawdust). However, Johnny had one more fact up his sleeve – that hard woodchips and sawdust were about three times heavier than the fluffy woodchips – 'So my tons would be quicker to deliver, and also as the hard wood was not completely suitable for the new type bales they would also make more rejects for me to buy cheap!'

It looked as if going skint wasn't on the cards just yet.

Johnny was well aware that the Dutch company had invested heavily in its English subsidiaries. You would hardly miss it. They put in their own fleet of lorries, about ten of them, all top of the range and very expensive. Added to that, some of them were equipped with a special vacuum system made to suck up the woodchips directly into the lorries which were designed to carry bulk instead of stacked up chips. The vacuum system was reversible so that it could blow the chips right near the bailing machine.

All very smart, modern and efficient, but gradually Johnny became aware that all was not as well as it may have seemed at the beginning. In the first place, the balers were operated by the mill owner's staff, who were not as interested in the output of the waste as they were in the milling of their own timber. Therefore, if the baler had problems for a day or so it didn't worry them, providing it didn't interfere with their mainstream business. But, of course, for the Dutch, with their heavy investment in lorries, balers, and so on it was vital that each plant was run efficiently.

It didn't take long for Johnny to notice all the problems at Phoenix. The stocks of bales built up for several reasons – firstly, not all of the local farmers were in the frame of mind to buy this new product. It was summer and they didn't need to stock up yet. Each plastic wrapped compressed bale was much heavier, about three times the weight of a sack of woodchips, and more expensive. Three sacks would have cost six shillings; the equivalent in weight – one bale – was eight shillings. Another daunting factor was that the lorry drivers would only deliver a full load because as the bales were regular size they were carried stackable and the transport could then carry more weight. So it meant the farmer had to buy a minimum of eight tons at a time, rather than four tons. Yet another thing limiting sales was that the firm did very little advertising.

Noting all this and knowing that he could do better, he offered to take the surplus off their hands and by the end of summer he certainly had shown them that it could be done. Having cleared their backlog by early winter, Johnny wanted to keep his hold on this company – so he and Marion took a trip to Holland to meet the two Dutch brothers.

'We spent two days of pretty hard bargaining and negotiating, but in the end a good work plan was devised,' he says. It was agreed that Johnny would be given a contract to run General Chip Co in the UK alongside his own company. Gerald Hart would be instantly disposed of, as with Johnny in charge there would be no need for a manager. The Dutch brothers and Johnny shook hands over the deal and he and Marion left to return home.

'I was quite excited over the deal with the Dutch men,' Johnny remembered, 'but on the way home crossing the North Sea on the ferry, Marion brought it to my attention that as the brothers were now instantly disposing of Gerald Hart and replacing him with me, although I was not employed by the Dutchmen, they now had no need of a manager they would – and could – dispose of me and my company just as quickly. Contract or no contract.'

At this moment, it only meant that Johnny would be watchful. Meanwhile it didn't take him long to turn General Chip from a loss making firm into a profit making company.

To ensure that his own company was not suffering any neglect while he was working for the Dutch Brothers, Johnny decided to promote one of his lorry drivers – an excellent, eager, hard worker called Ray Moss. The young man happily accepted the new responsibilities and very shortly Johnny crowned his diligence with the title of manager of the Inkster company.

Ray particularly liked the sales side and one of his favourite jobs was taking charge of the stand Johnny had taken for many years at the Essex Agricultural Show. The stand was shared with a turkey farmer who showed turkeys and was offering turkey breeding requirements and instructions. As in all county shows this stand also carried some entertainment for the public including coffee and sandwiches. The opportunity of running such a showpiece gave Ray a feeling of pride, especially when rubbing shoulders with the important people from big agricultural merchants and advertisers.

'Financially the stand was a success,' said Johnny. 'We took plenty of orders there, so I agreed to follow that by taking another stand at the annual Poultry Show in Hartford. And Ray would run it.'

This show also proved to be a success, so the enthusiastic young man, buoyed up by his achievements was in search of further excitement. 'Can I,' he asked, 'book us a stand for three to four days at the Royal Windsor Horse Show?'

There was no holding him, Johnny decided, and although he admired the youthful enthusiasm, had to draw a halt at this one. 'It's too dear,' he explained. 'More than a hundred pounds for the stand. Not this one, Ray.'

Ray was bitterly disappointed and sulked like a child, recalls Johnny, and didn't speak to anyone for over a week. Not even to Marion who noticed his silence and asked: 'What's up with the boy?' And when Johnny told her he wouldn't allow a stand at the Royal Windsor Show, she understood Ray's grief.

A week or two later, the young manager approached Johnny again and, in a serious, unsmiling voice said: 'I don't suppose it will matter to you, but the Royal International Horse Show at Wembley is coming soon. They have dozens of stands where they sell saddles, bridles, horse foods – many other things…' Not wishing to give the lad the hump again, Johnny agreed to take a stand there to advertise and show his own goods and it would be entirely in Ray's charge. Ray had always fancied himself as a horseman and admired the horsey set, so was off a few days before the opening date in his Land Rover with its trailer filled with newly painted advertising boards, tables and chairs and anything else needed to set up the stand. When the opening day arrived, he set off at six in the morning dressed in a smart country-style jacket and trousers. He arrived back that night full of stories of the day, which had begun with various competitions of horses competing in knock-out trials with the winners appearing on BBC Television.

Ray was in his element, meeting up with old friends and customers from other shows, and because of the stand he could feel he was part of the horse set. One evening this was proved to him – the Duke of Edinburgh was passing the stand and said 'Good evening' to Ray and shook his hand. Things could hardly get any better than that.

Late every evening – usually around eleven, Ray would turn up at *The Chippings* to retail the excitements of the day to Johnny and Marion.

'On about the second or third day of the show,' Johnny remembered, 'Ray told us about an amazing team of Hungarian horse riders. He said he had never seen anything like them. The team, called the Chikorsh Riders came from the central plains of Hungary and their act, performed in their native costumes, was amazing.

'One man, he told us, would ride bareback on five horses at the same time. Another carried a large whip which when cracked made a horse lay down still and one of the riders would stand on it. Another crack of the whip and the horse would sit up on its haunches like a dog.

'Young Ray was obviously pixilated by this equestrian team. They couldn't speak any English, but had an interpreter with whom he made friends.'

When the show ended – and it had also proved to be a financial success for Johnny's firm – Johnny and the family decided to take off on their boat to sail from the Solent to Torquay for a holiday.

'We had a great all-day trip down the coast,' said Johnny. 'After mooring the boat safely in Torquay, I slipped ashore hoping to catch a shop open to buy some treats for the kids and a newspaper for myself and Marion, so we could see what was happening in the rest of the world while we'd been offshore. While Marion made us a cup of tea, I sat reading the paper. Then my eye fell on a small story on an inside page…

'I called out to Marion: Here's a coincidence… and read the piece out to her. Strangely, it told of those Hungarian horse riders Ray had told us about. When the group left their last performance at Southsea, they packed into their horseboxes to make for Dover where they were to sail off for home. Two of the young riders, however, had jumped out of their box and had now vanished somewhere into the English countryside.

'We both read it a couple of times again, then put the paper away and forgot it.'

As soon as he got back from the Torquay holiday, Johnny was anxious to know what the work programme at his own company was likely to be for the next few days. On Monday he asked Bob the mechanic for a report, because Ray was not there. Bob gave him a run down. Someone had ordered a load of sawdust in sacks.

'Where for?' Johnny asked.

'The Phoenix Mill in Rainham. Ray has set the two boys to sack it up.'

'Two boys? What two boys?'

'Oh, the two Hungarian boys.'

Too much of a coincidence? He phoned Ray.

'Ah, yes... you mean Karoly Dora – we call him Karchie – and his brother, Josef Turi, known as Jorshka. They are busy right now sacking up the sawdust for Rainham. They are bloody good workers.'

'Where did they come from?'

'Jumped out of a horsebox in Hampshire.'

'Where do they live now?'

'In a caravan behind my cottage.'

'How did they get here from Southsea – to Stapleford Abbots in Essex – about a hundred miles and not an easy place to find?'

No answer. Change of subject. Just: 'They are both fit and well and bloody good workers.'

'What do you intend to do with them?'

'Keep them in the firm. They love it here. Kit [Ray's wife] took them shopping to Collier Row on Saturday and went to Tesco where they both bought thirty packets of crisps and sat on the pavement and ate them. They'd never seen so much food in one shop in all their lives.

'But there must have been something in the papers about them, or somebody reported on them, because the other day two men in bowler hats and smart suits arrived to question me. They were bloody abrupt and knew all about me – where I was born, went to school, where my parents live. They also knew all about you, Johnny. Knew your father had been a copper, knew which stations he had served at. Also all about your family – everything.'

Johnny asked him what he had said.

'I told them I liked the boys. That I'd first seen them at a horse show, then they jumped out of the horsebox because they didn't want to go home and that they were going to ask for asylum. I also told them they were bloody good workers.'

Special Branch or MI5 or whoever they were, had told Ray that the Hungarian government wanted them sent back, so Johnny told his young manager not to tell anybody they were in his caravan and that meanwhile they should apply for permission to stay in Britain by seeking asylum at Croydon.

'Ray brought the two boys to meet me and Marion. They appeared to be bewildered with the country, the amount of food in the shops, the choice of clothing, and our general standard of living,' he said. After a few days Marion applied to the Home Office for permission for them to stay, and learnt that the criterion was that they needed to have a job, but that they couldn't do a job that any unemployed Englishman could do. It was a real *Catch-22* situation – they couldn't stay unless there was a job for them, but it couldn't be a job that anybody else could do.

Johnny thought there may be a solution. He had a herd of Highland cattle and their calves in a field near his house, and a job specifically looking after the herd might be a way round the problem. There was only one way to find out. He first had to post a vacancy, then apply for a work permit at the local Labour Exchange for the Hungarians, then take them along in person to be interviewed.

Johnny sighed as he recollected the story. 'As we entered the office, I noticed there were several men and boys waiting – including one ginger-haired young layabout. I guessed they were after the vacancy I had specified.'

He and the two Hungarians were called into an office. The manager, a pompous chap, read the request for *two cowboys* and said: 'We don't have cowboys in England.'

Johnny was ready with some photographs of his Highland cattle to show him, but the manager was still not convinced he would need two cowboys and, anyway, what skills did these two have that an Englishman wouldn't have?

Johnny had asked Karchie to bring his whip with him, and suggested that the moment had come for him to crack it, but the boy hesitated, thinking this was not the place to do it – the office seemed too important a place.

'Go ahead, anyway. Crack it!' commanded Johnny.

The boy swung the whip over the heads and cracked it with a sound like a gunshot. 'The manager nearly fell off his chair,' said Johnny. The ginger layabout in the queue shouted 'Sod it' and ran out of the door. Other doors from other offices opened and heads appeared. The Hungarian boys looked bewildered, but Johnny was quite pleased with the pandemonium he was responsible for. In any event the manager appeared convinced that they were cowboys, as required, and agreed to accept the forms which were then sent to Croydon.

In a few weeks permission was granted for the two Hungarians to stay in England indefinitely. Marion taught them English in their spare time and they eventually became naturalised English citizens. The two lads who Johnny always said 'fell off a lorry' into his firm, continued to work with him until other ideas took their fancy and they moved on.

Now that his business worries were sorted out and both new and old organisations were running happily along, with Ray running one and himself supervising the other, Johnny had a little time to think about his family. And so began what he has since called his own personal Shaggy Dog Story….

It was now more than two years since Jennie was born, she would very soon be a toddler and Mark was nearing kindergarten age and Johnny thought the kids should have a pet. Johnny's ideas and his aspirations always came BIG. So, of course, the sort of pet he was looking for was a St Bernard. Big dogs, he thought (touching wood and crossing fingers) don't do much, are docile and affectionate, especially with children. (Remember Nana the gentle giant belonging to *Peter Pan*'s Wendy?) And as tubby, fluffy, tumbling puppies, they are adorable. So Nikki came to live with and be cuddled by the Inkster family for a few years. These dogs are not very long-lived, so Nikki was, sadly, eventually replaced by another of the same cuddly breed, called Samantha.

One of the problems of the St Bernard is that many admirers of the soft, fluffy balls of puppyhood do not realise, or willingly forget when they make the attractive toy-like puppy purchase, that the cute baby grows up to fill rather a lot of house-space and to have an appetite commensurate with the huge void of the giant dog's stomach. So, to rid themselves of this problem in the kindest possible way, the owner of one St Bernard will often contact the owner of another to ask if they would like to take their out-grown pet on board. So it was with Henry, a very large, fully-grown male. His present worn out squeezed up owners contacted Johnny and came over one Sunday afternoon, to inspect the premises, Deciding that the Inksters were suitable and willing owners for their about-to-be-discarded darling, and the house and grounds large enough to accommodate him, they invited Johnny to return to their home to see and, hopefully, pick up Henry.

All went very well, especially when Henry – a lover of cars – spotted Johnny's Rolls and jumped in to sprawl full-length along the ample back seat, as though to a Roller born. He became a good pet and got on well with Samantha.

Johnny realised one day after living with these two handsome beasts, that puppies from the pair could now raise about a hundred pounds each. Johnny and family were away on holiday when Samantha came into season, but clear and strict instructions had been left with the dogs' carer that if this should happen, Samantha and Henry should be locked in the barn together thus ensuring that should he have his way with her, any pups would be pedigree.

When Johnny and family returned from their holiday a few weeks later, they were delighted to hear that Samantha was in pup and as they had been locked in the barn together, it was assumed Henry was the father.

Eventually, Samantha went into a difficult labour, but assisted by a local vet was safely delivered of twelve live puppies. Curiously, all the pups were different, no two alike. Some were all white, some brown and white, some white with black eyes or black paws – only two of them in any way resembled their apparent St Bernard parents. Johnny queried this with the vet, who gave his opinion that this all-sorts variety often occurred with highly bred pairs, but that in the breeding business, the professional breeder would no doubt have some of the odd ones put down immediately.

'That's not an option with us,' Johnny announced firmly, and all twelve pups were reared.

When the traditional weaning and rearing period was ending, an advertisement was put in *Exchange and Mart,* the family's favourite paper for buying or selling.

The ad offered St Bernard puppies at £100 each. And immediately the telephone started ringing. People arrived from all over the country to see the twelve delightful balls of fluff gambolling over the stable floor. Amazingly the oddly marked pups sold first, leaving the best until last.

The first hint of trouble came from a nurse recently retired from a London hospital. When her dog was about four months old, she took it to the vet for an inoculation. The vet eyed her pet quizzically and asked: 'What kind of a dog is it?'

Surprised, and wondering what kind of a vet he was not to know, she said: 'A St Bernard, of course.' At which the vet fell about roaring with laughter. The nurse then produced the pedigree form Johnny had made out and given her. The vet looked it over and pronounced it rubbish.

The nurse was not worried about her pet or its bastard breed, but was concerned about the pedigree. She telephoned Johnny and told him of the vet's disbelief.

Johnny immediately offered to take the pup back and give her a full refund, but she would not part with the dog she had become fond of.

The second puppy sold had been all white with black patches over its eyes, and Johnny had named it Bill Sykes, because he looked like a burglar. A publican from Lincolnshire was very taken with him and paid the hundred pound fee for dog and pedigree. Eventually a letter came from the publican saying that Bill Sykes had grown into a marvellous dog and he was delighted with his purchase, but there had been some queries about the breed, not only from several teasing customers, but also from the local vet. In defence he had framed the pedigree and hung it up in the pub for all to see. His letter was in no way a complaint, but he would like to know what the breed actually was. Johnny replied that the birth of the pups had been attended by a vet with high qualifications, and could vouch for the validity of the breed. No more was heard.

As more complaints or enquiries came in, Johnny had a word with the dog-carer who had been in charge while the family was away on holiday. 'Did you actually see the mating?'

'Well – er – no,' the man admitted and confessed that; 'one morning when I arrived, I found the stable door open and Samantha was in there with the half-breed Alsatian from the scrap-yard next door.'

A few days later the vet called round to see the family and the remaining pups and Johnny tackled him on the subject.

'Of course they aren't pure-bred St Bernards,' he said, 'but I could see you and your wife were worried, and in my view it is the duty of a vet attending an animal to reassure the owner's mind, just in case the worst should happen and the dog dies. I also hope that other vets feel the same sense of duty when a new owner takes the puppy for an inoculation, or whatever. And when the question of breed comes up will say: What a beautiful specimen'.

Johnny was not quite sure the vet's comments had set his mind at rest, especially a few days later when a solicitor's letter arrived from one of the pup's owners, a lady in Devon. Several letters had already been received from this owner; usually giving updates on the dog's weight, dietary milestones, and lengths of enjoyable moorland walks together. The solicitor's letter, however, told a different story. 'It is thanks to you,' the legal gentleman complained, 'that my client has become the laughing stock of the village,' and a full refund of the purchase price was being sought.

Bearing in mind the latest information he had received on the possible ancestry of the puppies he had in all innocence sold, Johnny thought the best thing to do now was to confess and make the offer of a full refund on return of the dog.

The solicitor replied that his lady client wished to know what would become of her pet if it were returned for the refund. Johnny replied sadly that it was extremely hard to place a fully-grown St Bernard and thus only the vivisection labs would take him.

At this news the case was quietly dropped and the lady owner was never heard from again.

In view of all these problems, however, and now with the knowledge that Samantha had jilted her handsome Henry and sewn her wild oats with the bit of rough from the scrapyard nearby, Johnny decided to give up being a breeder himself, but was ready to save Henry's face by putting him out to stud. Suddenly the pedigree sire was in clover at £50 a time. No end of beautiful bitches – nearly all of them called Nana - were produced for his delight.

The stud business, Johnny found, also had its tribulations. One of the first customers telephoned to ask if he could drop off his bitch, newly in season, early in the morning on his way to work in the city.

'No problem,' Johnny assured him, knowing that Henry was always ready and willing for a new affair.

The canine couple greeted each other with mounting interest and were taken into the barn where they were locked in and left to pursue their mating in private. Around teatime Johnny went to the barn to see how things were shaping.

Shock, horror! History repeating itself, the barn door was swinging open, the bitch was gone and her lover was sound asleep. There was no time to wonder whether the deed had been done, a posse had to be organised to find and retrieve the vanishing lady.

Search parties sought high and wide and long, but with no result and panic was beginning to settle on the shoulders of the home party manning the telephone so that they could control events if the bitch was discovered on the run. But the worst call came late in the evening from the owner to say he was about to leave the office and would call for his pet on the way home. Johnny took over.

'Well, we think it would be an idea to leave the pair together for the night. It – er – took them quite a while to get acquainted, so to ensure success, I think a night together might clinch the deal. Ok?'

Of course the owner agreed, so they had twenty-four hours extra to find the missing bitch and try to secure a successful mating. The searches went on until nearly dark with no happy result. By around four in the afternoon of the next day, panic had reached a high level. The local police had been alerted for lost dogs. The yellow pages had been searched for the veterinary personnel in the vicinity and telephoned to see whether run-over dogs had been reported to them. How could you lose a St. Bernard?

Despairing, the team was working out how – and what – to tell the bitch's owner when he called that night, when the local Esso rep who sold diesel for Johnny's lorries called in.

'What's up?' he asked, sensing the atmosphere. Johnny explained the reason for the panic, and the problem.

The man pushed back his cap and thought for a moment. 'Here,' he said. 'I saw a big dog like one of your St Bernards just up the road mating with an Alsatian. D'ye think that would be it?'

But there was no one there to answer his question. The posse had left to round up its quarry.

The escapee was captured and put back with Henry – in hope – until her owner picked her up later. Perhaps if any resulting litter turned out to be as multi-coloured as Samantha's had been, the vet, remembering his kind duty, would reassure the owner that pedigree St Bernards often looked like that at birth, and that these were wonderful specimens. Or, that maybe Henry had indeed got there

114

first. Johnny never found out, and certainly wasn't going to risk asking.

One winter's evening a young couple arrived with their Nana to be served. The courting lawn was drenched with rain, and the lady owner stood with her heels sinking into the sodden grass holding Nana, very much in season, on a strong lead as Johnny went to let the ever-eager suitor out of his kennel. The big boy bounded over and jumped on the young bitch who was not used to this Essex-style courting; she yelped and ran off, dragging her owner, high-heels, fur coat and all, through the mud.

Henry, his desire abounding, saw the mud-covered furry thing and, possibly thinking it was another St Bernard, leaped upon the sprawling woman. Johnny, in hasty recognition of what the intentions of his randy pet were, jumped quickly to the rescue and pulled the reluctant Henry away.

When the woman's partner had put her back on her heels, blotted off some of the mud and peace was somewhat restored, Johnny suggested they take Henry home with them for his night of passion so that Nana might feel happier in the familiar surroundings of her own home. The young couple greeted the idea happily and the two great dogs were squeezed in and lashed down into their very small car. Two days later they returned Henry with whom they – and Nana – had fallen in love.

Chapter Seven
Problems with Plywood.

After his brief flirtation with dog breeding, Johnny returned to his long love affair with wood. As Marion had predicted when he first took the job, he began to feel his job as manager to the Dutch owned General Chip Company was not as permanently secure as he had once imagined. Things began to unwind when one of his own team who had originally been hired as a lorry driver, an excellent young chap called Ray Moss, who worked like a trooper, was promoted by Johnny himself within his company. This, apparently, had been noted by the Dutch Brothers who then 'head hunted' him themselves and replaced Johnny with Ray as manager.

This didn't do much for the friendship between Johnny and Ray Moss, but after a long estrangement it was eventually patched up.

In the meantime, of course, Johnny had his eye on the building world and noticed that chipboard, with which he had by now been associated for some time, was being accompanied by plywood and decorative wallboard made from plywood and this was finding a huge and appreciative audience in the building and furniture trades. Although neither sawdust nor wood chips played any part in this new product, it was still wood, so Johnny was interested. The new plywood, made from wood veneers glued together, might well have rejects that, as in the chipboard and the baling business, he could buy up cheap and sell at a profit to the builders and the do-it-yourself customers who were finding plywood very expensive.

But, as things turned out, it was not going to be as easy as that. There were no manufacturers of plywood in the United Kingdom at that time – it all came from abroad, from countries where there were wood-production forests, such as United States, Canada, Russia and the Far East.

Johnny sighed, rejects might not be possible in plywood; they might be all gobbled up in their country of manufacture or difficult, or impossible, to export to England. History was also against him. During the war all imports of raw materials had been controlled and rationed. This had created a culture of exclusive importers – that is, only the ones who had originally imported via a government licence.

Percy had told him: 'It's no good, Johnny, thinking you can import plywood, or anything else without a licence. In fact, I was keen to import timber, so I took the only way – bought up a licensed import company, in order to do it.'

As always, Johnny was not one to accept defeat without a fight, so he made enquiries around the trade. 'It appeared,' he said, 'that all the controls had long since gone – it was only the culture that remained – so I resolved to cut through it.'

He decided that he would get more change from the Far Eastern exporters on what he was looking for, than from the Americans, Russians or Canadians. Anyway, he would initially investigate the Far East. His first move was to telephone the trade departments of the various embassies in London for the addresses of the manufacturers in each country. Telex at the time was the cutting edge of technology, and he sent messages to the addresses he had obtained. Several replies came back, one from a man called Tham Kwok Onn, a Chinese Singaporean who

117

specialised in exporting hard wood and plywood to Europe. He telephoned back to Johnny.

'I like to ask,' he said, 'what you mean by Reject? I ask because if I send something you do not like, or do not want, you have no protection. It cannot be returned, you have lost your money.' He pointed out that good quality material was of course warranted by various country trade associations. But he did not understand the word Rejects.

Johnny explained that it meant not top quality; it could even be damaged or water-stained. He understood, as importer, he would in that case have no redress or guarantee. He decided that Tham Kwok Onn sounded a pretty honest bloke, so suggested he sent him a list of what he had that was not his first class stuff. Tham's reply, immediately telexed, was a long list of plywood described as 'Old stock, some very dusty, some with various imperfections, some soiled, some water-stained'.

Tham added that if this was the sort of material Johnny wanted, he could comply, but would need an 'Irrevocable letter of credit' from a bank. Johnny had no idea what that was, or what it meant. It was beginning to look as if it wasn't going to be a piece of cake. It seemed that to import anything you needed documents about which he knew nothing. Tham's 'irrevocable letter of credit' from the bank was just the first document.

Johnny said: 'My next move was to go to see my bank manager, who it appeared hadn't a clue, either. He had never completed such a document, so we sat at his desk with a book of regulations and worked out what to do. The form was pretty complicated, it consisted first of the seller's name and address and the buyers name and address.

'Then, *Question*: Would I, the buyer, allow the LC (letter of credit) to be traded and sold on for someone else to complete the order? *Answer*: No, I would not. *Question*:

Would I buy f.o.b (free on board) or c.i.f. (carriage, insurance and freight) to UK? *Answer*: I – hopefully – chose c.i.f. *Question*: Would I allow the seller to get the cheapest transhipment? It would not then come direct to England. *Answer*: No. *Question*: Give a very accurate description of the goods as, if the goods did not conform to this description, the banks would not pay in London, or in Singapore. *Answer*: How to describe Reject? (My bank manager said maybe we should just use the word Reject because Tham's invoice recently received by airmail on rice paper had the word stamped in large letters all over it. But – if I did, I would have no rights at all.) We decided to describe them as Reject anyhow.'

After his bank manager had also explained 'bill of laden', the other document he had to produce for this overseas shipment, Johnny contacted Tham Kwok Onn and ordered six thousand pounds worth of the rejects Tham had described.

Tham Kwok Onn was a pretty fast worker once the money was on the way and it wasn't long before Johnny's first shipment of plywood rejects was loaded onto a cargo ship called *Borsumi* bound for Tilbury. As this was the first time he had bought from overseas, Johnny was anxious to know the progress of 'his' ship. One of his boating mates who had been in the Merchant Navy and knew about the movement of ships at sea told him if he bought a copy of England's oldest newspaper called *Lloyd's Register of Shipping* (known as *Lloyd's List*), he would be able to follow the *Borsumi*'s progress.

'I monitored the ship all the way' Johnny enthused, 'via the heavy broadsheet pages of the paper. I read when it passed through the Suez Canal and read of it passing Gibraltar. Eventually, I felt the thrill of seeing the actual date of its arrival in Tilbury.'

119

Fascinated by this new venture, Johnny went himself to the docks the day after the *Borsumi* arrived. 'But no port official or docker had heard of my ship from Singapore, and nor had the security people who had allowed my entry as an importer. So I began to wonder whether it had sprung a leak somewhere along the line and had failed to keep its expected arrival date. Nobody seemed to have heard of it, or was very interested, so I decided to do a dockside search for myself.'

He drove around the port, checking all the names lettered on the shining hulls and the stern quarters of dozens of splendid container and cargo ships but nothing spelt out the name he was looking for, until – at last – he found it, in one corner, a curious battered rust-bucket moored alongside some of the gleaming painted hulls of elegant cargo vessels from all over the world. And – there she was, the *Borsumi* from Singapore, ready for discharging the contents of her hold and open decks.

Armed with his sheaf of all the correct papers, he found his plywood would be unloaded in about twenty-four hours, and then he could arrange for his own lorries to transport all his overseas cargo of rejects back to *The Chippings*. He was originally told that import duty was payable on all far eastern plywood, but when his bill of laden was lodged with customs there was nothing about duty on rejected plywood, only on various quality imports, so it was decided that his goods could be released duty free – saving him another ten percent overall.

'You know how it is when you order a Chinese meal,' Johnny said when telling the story to his coffee-rounds farmer friends, 'there always seems to be far more than you thought you had ordered – or could eat. Well, it was the same here. I think Tham Kwok Onn had used the opportunity to get rid of a lot of rejects he couldn't dispose of in Singapore, or find any other use for. There seemed to be almost twice what I'd paid for.'

And it all looked very good, and sold quickly, at three or four times the price paid, and as Tham's rejects were a nice little earner, Johnny immediately placed another order and continued to do so as it became available for several years. In time the Americans and Canadians also telexed offers of rejects and, having gained confidence in his dealings, he placed orders from the Southern States and also Canada.

'It all goes to show,' said Johnny, 'that if you think around a problem, you can usually find a way to solve it. Besides, to me it has always been fun. Everybody involved in the plywood deal also thought it was fun. Tham Kwok Onn thought it was fun, the bank manager thought it was fun; it's possible even the customs people might have thought it was fun. And that's the way I've always worked.'

That was the beginning of Johnny's venture into the plywood business – but it was by no means the end. As time went on, plywood boards were perfected by a new special process. A photograph was taken of a piece of timber and then transposed onto a sheet of thin plywood. V-shaped grooves were cut into the surface of the board to give the appearance of real timber planking and a melamine coating applied to it gave a hardwearing, washable surface. Wallboard was coming of age and was popular with all builders and furniture manufacturers – especially for new 'luxury' kitchen and bedroom fittings.

Johnny was expanding his own business to trading in rejects of the wallboards and also the furniture rejects made from them. He dealt mainly with timber firms who were dealing in both. One such firm run by the Silverman family was called Coronet Timber Ltd and their business was in Hoxton Square, on the northern (Shoreditch) borders of London's East End. Johnny and the Silvermans had a lot in common; like him they traded in bankrupt stocks and fire damaged timber and one day Johnny heard they had acquired a large stock of wallboards from a fire.

As the boards were in packs and tightly packed in sheathing ply, the flames had only just touched the sides when the fire brigade had hosed them down. This, of course, created water-damaged boards and some had been charred, so all these had to be thrown away. Some, however, were in very good condition. All the rest, even the fire scorched ones, were saleable at a knock-down price. The Silverman family had no great luck in finding buyers as they were, after all, basically suppliers to the trade and like most people in the timber trade at that time they did not deal directly with the public. But now they were eager to get rid of this untidy stock, especially as the boards needed sorting and were cluttering up their premises.

When Johnny heard about the problem, he stepped in quickly and after a bit of negotiation offered eight shillings a board, delivered to him at *The Chippings*. The family was happy to get rid of this otherwise useless stock and Johnny was happy as he knew he would be able to sell at two pounds fifty a board to the general public.

A couple of weeks later two men in a lorry loaded with ten tons of wallboards – a different colour and a different make – turned up at *The Chippings* and asked for Johnny. They were offering to sell him their boards.

'Hey, don't I know you?' Johnny asked one of the men. 'Aren't you a lorry driver for Charlie the plywood dealer?'

'I was once,' the man said, 'but not now. I'm setting up in business for myself. And I'm selling plywood.' The boards he was offering looked in good condition, new, but slight seconds with marks on some of the surfaces, splits and pin worm holes on the backsides, and he wanted a pound each for them.

'Too dear,' said Johnny. 'I've got a large stock anyway, and they only cost me eight bob each. However, I'm prepared to make you an offer – yours for the same price – eight bob a board.' But the two men shook their heads and drove off.

Some time later in the same day they returned saying they had had no luck selling their boards, so would now accept the eight shilling offer.

Johnny considered it. He had a pretty large stock anyway, but the price was cheap, especially for the brand new, unused boards. 'Are they your own boards? Or some of Charlie's you're flogging for him?'

The man shook his head. 'No, they're not Charlie's or anyone else's – they're mine.'

Nevertheless, Johnny asked the man to come to his office and sign a paper to say the wallboards were his to sell. He was obeying an instinct that he had learnt from the motor trade where it was standard procedure. Car dealers used this practice to stop people trying to sell cars they had on hire purchase and were actually owned by the finance houses.

Once he had the signature, Johnny paid for the ten tons by cheque. The man asked if Johnny could arrange for it to be cashed.

'No problem,' said Johnny and telephoned to his bank to make arrangements. The sum was about two thousand, eight hundred pounds. The bank manager was amenable and, after unloading the boards the man went off with his friend to present the cheque.

Johnny advertised the boards along with the fire-charred products in the *London Evening News*, and they began to sell straight away.

A few miles away lived a farmer called Brian whose brother worked with him on their farm and between them they were making a living, but only just. They had been looking out for some other way of increasing their income and had appealed to Johnny. Johnny, was as helpful as he could be to Brian and his wife who were old friends, and he knew them to be honourable people who were trying to earn enough to renovate their cottage. He offered them the opportunity of selling some of his boards on a sale-or-return basis.

'My only condition,' he told them, 'is that you don't advertise them in London, and just sell locally, so you don't cut across my trade.' It was agreed and next day Johnny delivered a good stack of boards for the brothers to sell. Brian managed to build up a good local trade and happily was able to supplement the income from his farm. Within a short time he had a lot of luck selling the boards to local council estates and was eventually making around a hundred pounds a week – about four times the average working man's wages at that time.

A few weeks later Johnny was on one of his coffee-round tours and dropped in to Richard Fowler's farm. Richard was Charterhouse-educated and had a big Essex farm, but was tired of farming, tired of work and tired of the present government. That evening, Johnny and Richard were busy putting the world to rights when a phone call to Johnny came from Marion.

'Your farmer friend Brian has just been on the telephone asking for you,' she told him, 'and he's in a bit of a state. At the moment he's surrounded by police and he and his brother have been arrested. The Flying Squad claim that the wall boards have been stolen and want to know where they got them. They mentioned they came from you. The cops didn't seem to think much of that for an answer. So could you please pop over and reassure them?'

'I'll phone there first,' Johnny replied, 'and find out what's going on.'

Brian's wife, answered. 'We've got the Flying Squad here,' she told him, trying to sound calm. 'And the dock police of the Port of London Authority...' Johnny interrupted her to take over and asked to speak to one of the officers.

When the policeman came to the phone he introduced himself as Detective Inspector George, and asked: 'Did you sell this load of wallboards to Brian? If so, I want you to come and see me.'

Johnny was only a few miles away from Brian's farm, so he left immediately to drive over and within a short time was at the scene of the alleged crime – whatever it was. He was a bit shocked on arrival to see how many police officers were there – four or five from the Flying Squad, several unmarked police cars and one local panda car with a policeman whose greeting was 'Hello, Johnny – I don't know what all this is about'.

Johnny explained that as far as he knew the boards were not stolen. 'I know my responsibilities as a dealer,' he said. 'I bought them properly from a man I knew, not a stranger I had met in a pub.' To the police hoping to make an arrest, Johnny was giving them all the 'wrong' answers.

'How much did you pay for them?'

He told them honestly and frankly.

'How do you sell them?'

'Via advertisements in the *Evening News.*'

The policeman from the London docks – another detective inspector – obviously wanted a quick arrest, but Inspector George, perhaps being more experienced, felt their case was getting messed up.

'Why is the plywood all hidden under those tarpaulins?'

'It is not hidden,' Johnny replied. 'It's covered to keep it dry, if it rains.'

'Why have you left it in the crate with the markings on?'

'Only to keep it clean.'

Inspector George was not happy with Johnny's answers; the situation was not going his way. The docks cop was wanting somebody nicked.

Earlier when they had arrested Brian and his brother for 'dishonestly handling stolen goods', Brian's reply had been: 'Fair enough, mate, but I've got to keep feeding my animals.'

The dock officer had replied: 'You can't feed them – you are under arrest.'

But the better Inspector George had butted in: 'For Christ's sake, let him feed his animals – we've got enough troubles.'

When Johnny later heard of this dialogue, he knew what it all meant. George was certainly no fool, Johnny's policeman father had told him it was always complicated to arrest people who had animals. It was the police's responsibility to inform the RSPCA or arrange for some similar animal welfare organisation to take over and care for animals belonging to an arrested person. And it was always complicated and took time.

Now, as the two brothers were escaping immediate arrest because of their farm animals, the docks D.I. wanted a further arrest. The Flying Squad appeared satisfied with Johnny's explanation of how he had acquired the boards and explained to him what had happened to alert the police. The goods had been picked up from the docks with a forged bill of laden.

'It sometimes happens,' the Flying Squad man told him, 'that the trader who has ordered the goods from overseas is not the man who picks them up or has the original bill of laden. It's fairly traditional. You see, if the goods –

126

whatever they are – are on a long journey, the trader spends the transport time by selling off what he has ordered. Thus, bills of laden would then be exchanged, so a different person would pick them up, instead of the original owner.'

Johnny explained that when he bought the boards he had seen both the bill of laden and the invoice. He then invited the police team back to *The Chippings* where he showed them the cheque book stub indicating that he had indeed bought the boards from a chap who he had known as a driver for another plywood dealer. The police were also shown his supply of the newer boards matching those held by the farming brothers – they all had the brand name of Honey boards and Johnny had advertised them with that name.

It turned out that there was only one importer of Honey boards in England, a company in Bow. When the Bow company manager had seen Johnny's advertisements in the *Evening News* at a price well below their own sale-price, he was immediately suspicious. He checked their stocks held in the docks and found some were missing. When another advertisement for Honey boards also appeared in the Romford paper, the Bow company asked the newspaper to name the advertiser and had gone to Brian's and discovered what appeared to be a supply of their missing goods. The Flying Squad was then alerted and the dock police informed.

The Flying Squad officers decided Johnny was innocent. They couldn't believe he would deal in stolen goods, then use the trade name to advertise them for sale.

But even that did not satisfy the inspector from the dock police and Johnny was arrested for dishonest handling and taken off with the brothers to Limehouse police station where the dock inspector ordered the station sergeant to take them to the cells.

'No can do,' the sergeant replied. 'There are no keys for the cells.'

The dock man nearly exploded at this news, but Inspector George butted in trying to smooth things over. 'They're not likely to do a runner. Let them sit on that bench there.'

Obediently, the three 'suspects' sat patiently while they were booked and eventually all three were charged with dishonestly handling stolen goods and released on bail to appear in Harbour Square police court next morning.

Chapter Eight
The Court Case

Although charged with a serious crime, Johnny was confident that his own honest trading would be believed. But he was surprised, daunted and somewhat depressed when the bails were set. The two brothers were bailed at two hundred pounds each. His bail was four thousand! Why? Did the police regard him as the ringleader of a gang of thieves and even forgers?

It appeared that the Honey boards could only have been obtained by a forged bill of laden. Innocent though he knew himself to be, it was possible that an innocent man could be found guilty. It had happened before, he knew, and it could happen again. He also knew that the size of his bail would attract a story in his local paper, and this in its turn could prove costly to his reputation and might even flush out damaging gossip, whether true or false, about him, his family and friends.

With these thoughts in his mind, Johnny was tempted to fight the case himself, especially as he couldn't bring any friendly lawyer's name to mind. However, Marion talked him out of that venture.

'You don't know enough about the law,' she told him. 'You need a good solicitor and a barrister to defend you.' He could only agree that she was right; however, there was no time to contact a solicitor before attending the police court next morning.

Once there, the only course he could think of (as some years before he had advised his innocent friend Dick

'Oxygen' Lewis), was to plead not guilty, reserve his defence and ask to go to trial. The two brothers decided to follow his example and go to trial.

On his way home from the court, Johnny was searching his memory for the name of a solicitor he knew, but had never used. It suddenly occurred to him – Alan Moore – a lad he had been at school with and who had eventually qualified as a solicitor and practiced locally. That was the chap. He'd known Johnny, or known of him, for many years, and would possibly appreciate something more interesting than the divorces, wills and conveyancing he was most probably handling at the moment. He made an early appointment and called at his old friend's office. Johnny told him the whole story and took along all the supporting paperwork he had.

The young lawyer was a little abashed when he heard the proposal; he explained that he had appeared in both civil and criminal court cases, but confessed: 'It will be my first case relating to receiving stolen goods... I've never defended anybody on this type of offence before, but don't worry. I'll ask one of the senior partners to recommend a barrister.' Johnny insisted that they should find a good criminal barrister who would do a worthy defence and get the case thrown out, obviously proving his own protested innocence.

Some days later he heard that the solicitor had approached a character called Michael West – and character he certainly was. An appointment was made for Alan Moore and Johnny to call at West's chambers in Kings Bench Walk in the Temple, London.

'It was a new experience for me,' Johnny later admitted. 'Something I had never known about, or even thought about. When you drive into the Temple, you are saluted – solicitors, barristers, criminals, murderers – all alike. And you are suddenly in a two-hundred year old village. It's

130

bloody interesting. The chambers are old and dusty. We were taken upstairs in this old, old house where Michael West worked when not in court. We were shown into a room no bigger than a toilet.

'He had obviously just returned from court, wearing pin-striped trousers and a barrister's collar. And he didn't look at all like I had expected my barrister would look. He had long, black, curly hair – which I supposed went under a wig in court – and thick pebble-lens specs. He made us some tea in a dirty old kettle and offered biscuits. It was the worst tea I had ever tasted.

'Then Michael West began to cross-examine me. Roughly, really. Every question I answered, he tried another to trip me up. He had obviously read up all about the case from the notes the police had supplied him with. He really hammered me, treating me as if I was guilty. It seemed to go on all the afternoon.'

Before he was satisfied, West asked Johnny whether the police had tried to bribe him.

'Not really,' Johnny told him, 'but there had been one police constable at the station who said if I pleaded guilty, I would only be fined a hundred pounds and be finished with at the police court next day.

Eventually, after more probing questions, Michael West's heated blood-red face twisted into a smile. 'Yes,' he said, 'I'll defend you. Go and see my clerk and get my fee.'

It was then that Johnny realised this defence might be very costly. West could easily have seen that Johnny was not a gullible type, not easy to be taken in.

The woman clerk told him the fees would be two hundred and fifty pounds a day, plus seventy five pounds for that day's briefing.

Johnny mulled this over. 'But I naturally wanted to know what the whole case was likely to cost me, so I asked how long she thought the case would last at two-hundred-and-fifty a day. She must have handled enough cases to be able to give some sort of rough estimate. But she just shrugged and said it could go to a week or more. Nobody could tell.

'So I came back with what I thought was a fair offer. A one-off fee of eight hundred pounds plus the seventy-five for that day's briefing. Plus a hundred pounds cash in the event the case was thrown out by the judge and didn't go to a jury.

'My thinking was that for a top class criminal lawyer like West, this case could be done with one hand tied behind his back.'

But the clerk's tart reply had been: 'You are hardly in a position to negotiate, Mr Inkster.' To which she received Johnny's retort that on his way to the Temple he had seen a lot of barristers looking thin and worried.

When the matter of the fee was settled, Johnny returned to West's office to find out where and when the case was likely to be heard.

The answer to the 'where' question really shook Johnny. 'The Old Bailey – and my clerk will let you know when,' the barrister replied, coolly.

'The – the Old Bailey!' Johnny stuttered. He didn't like to mention it, but wasn't that the place where violent criminals, armed robbers. terrorists and notorious murderers were tried?

'The Bailey,' West replied. 'Oh yes, better a small chicken in a big shed than a big chicken in a small shed. The judge would no doubt like this case.' He looked on top of the world, mentally rubbing his hands at the idea of a quick, simple and lucrative dismissal.

John departed deep in thought. He assumed – and hoped – that perhaps Michael West knew that the case was cut and dried. He also realised that West was probably happy it was the Old Bailey because it was convenient for him being just around the corner, as it were, from the Temple.

It was nearly a year before Johnny heard from Michael West again when the clerk telephoned to summon him to the chambers for another meeting. He was given another cup of tea and a further grilling even more hostile and severe than before. He also heard that the two brothers had obtained legal aid to acquire their barrister about whom West showed his great delight. 'Their barrister is not great,' he said, 'but I'm not worried. I will conduct the defence and will ask for you to be put in the dock with the others.'

A further six months or so later, during which there was a legal silence, Johnny's solicitor Alan Moore, telephoned to say that the case would be called in a week or two, and that it had been confirmed it was to be in an Old Bailey court, but owing to the fact the historic old building was being renovated, cases were being heard in an old house in St James's Square.

Johnny couldn't decide whether to be glad or sorry that he was not going into one of the docks in London's famous, ancient, Central Criminal Court where cases far worse than his had been heard since 1539. However, when the day came for his trial, a great deal had been done to convert the interior of the old house into a proper court, complete with a dock, a suitable area for the twelve jury members, a proper bench for the judge overlooking the court and seats for prosecution and defence counsels. There was even a cell to hold the prisoners and it was here Johnny and the others surrendered bail and were told not to leave.

'When the case started,' Johnny recalled, 'for the first time I saw the law from the inside. It is bloody good theatre. The plot is devised by the criminals and the police and barristers are the stars. Oh, they were the best days of my life!'

Johnny took his place in the dock with the other prisoners, Brian the farmer and his brother and also the young man from whom Johnny had bought the Honey boards and the friend who had accompanied him for the sale. They had both been charged with theft. Johnny and the two brothers had been charged with dishonest handling of the stolen goods, which meant that when buying something, if asked, you must know who owned it, where it came from and what you were going to do with it.

Johnny's defence to that charge would be that he knew the boards had come from the docks; he knew the man from whom he bought them; he had not paid cash and had documents relating to the ownership of the boards he was buying.

He had tried objecting to West putting him in the same dock with the man and his friend from whom he had bought the boards but West had told him he wanted the jury to see the villains who had set Johnny up – and how different he was from them.

The proceedings began with the jury being sworn in. Michael West had said that he could object to any juror he didn't like, but he didn't wish to do that. The young man and his driver friend had two different barristers who both objected to many of the jurors.

The prosecution took the rest of that first day to set out the whole case. The boards were proved to exist. Johnny, as defendant, could have asked for the whole shipment to be brought into the court, but it was agreed that a sample of ten boards would be housed at the back of the court for reference.

The next day Detective Inspector George gave evidence. As part of Johnny's defence was that he had bought the boards cheaply because they were rejects, the inspector was asked by West if he knew they were rejects.

'No,' said George.

'Are you an underpaid, overworked policeman?' West asked.

'Yes.'

'When you have your house decorated, how do you pay the decorator?'

'I don't,' said George. 'I do it myself.'

'Ah, so you are a do-it-yourself man?' West continued.

'Yes.'

West then asked the inspector to inspect the boards. A court usher was asked to bring one forward. He tried to lift one, but he staggered and fell with it, moaning that he had injured his back. Johnny, without thinking, slipped out of the dock before the warder could stop him, picked up the heavy board and carried it to the front of the court – at which there was pandemonium. Johnny should not have left the dock, the prison officer should have restrained him. Johnny should not have approached the judge with the board, nor handled the evidence. The judge stilled the hubbub and restored order in the courtroom and smoothed everything over. Once the police inspector had examined the board and agreed it had imperfections, Johnny took the board back to its original place and returned to the dock.

Meanwhile, during this episode and later, Johnny noticed that there was one man in the front row of the jury who was loving it all, and every time West scored a point in Johnny's favour, the juror gave Johnny a sly wink and a thumbs-up sign. Johnny fervently hoped neither judge nor prosecution lawyers would notice this, for they might suspect there was some collusion going on.

The next witness for the prosecution was the dock police inspector, who did not perform well under West's cross-examination. Day two ended with the prosecution barrister grilling Johnny as to why, if he knew the goods were not stolen, did he ask his co-accused to sign that they were not. Johnny's reply was to produce an extract from a Ford dealership book, showing that Ford car dealers asked every seller of second-hand cars to confirm that the vehicle they were offering was their own, that is, not stolen. Johnny pointed out that in his case the principle was the same.

Further thumbs-up from the juror as it appeared the prosecution was about to close its case.

But there was still another important witness for the prosecution who was, of course, the original importer of the alleged stolen Honey boards. After being sworn in and giving his name and address, he told how he had concluded that the boards had been stolen. One of his salesmen had been questioned as to why his price was higher than the price of the same boards being advertised in the *Evening News*. When the owner heard this news, he began to make enquiries and later heard there were also Honey boards being advertised in the Romford paper. From there he traced the seller to the farmer Brian and his brother and after checking with the docks that the rest of his import had been removed by bills of laden not supplied by him, he informed the police.

Asked by one of the prosecution lawyers how he knew the boards advertised were his, he replied that he was the sole seller of Honey boards – they would all be stamped with that name.

Under examination and cross-examination he said that he always imported first class seconds and good rejects. He agreed that his loads were usually mixed but could not say whether this one was mixed or not – they had all been removed by thieves before he could see them. He agreed that the samples held in the court as evidence were very likely to be his.

The case for the defence began on the third day. As the participants arrived in court, it was noticed that all the ten sample reject boards had been replaced by twenty perfect boards. Johnny had said from the beginning that the boards the farmer brothers held were totally supplied by him – and those said by the prosecution to be stolen were, in fact, rejects of the second quality. In most cases it was obvious – they were just marbled. But like many 'seconds' some looked perfect, with maybe only a little pin wormhole on the back. It had occurred to Johnny, when he first saw the Honey boards the young man offered, that the original importer had rejected them and had offered them at a sale price. But what was this not-very-random selection doing here now?

He remembered that at the time of the arrests the police had taken a lorry load of the brothers' boards as evidence. And since it was deemed not necessary to bring all the lorry load into court, the prosecution asked West if he would agree to there only being ten boards – chosen at random, of course – from the lorry as exhibits of evidence. West saw no reason not to agree, and during the prosecution days this had certainly been the case. But now, the defence was about to begin – and different boards had been produced.

Johnny asked the driver who had delivered the boards that morning, why he had brought these particular samples. The man told him he had been up half the night until twenty *perfect* boards were located.

As they were entering the court, Johnny relayed this information to West who charged towards the prosecution benches and shouted, yelled, screamed and threatened the two opposing barristers that if those boards were not removed immediately, he would have all ten tons of boards brought to the court and spread out across St James's Square. Johnny had never seen anyone so angry, and when the court opened West's first move was to complain that the evidence had been tampered with.

Then he put Johnny up for cross-examination after dealing with his own questions to set the scene. It appeared that neither of the prosecution counsel was going to bring up the matter of the boards. Johnny was doing quite well at parrying their various attempts at attack when he noticed that the dock police inspector was getting quite agitated at Johnny's calm success and was feeding the prosecuting counsel with more and more questions. At this, Johnny suggested to the judge that the barrister and the dock inspector go somewhere else to whisper together as the policeman was interrupting the flow of the questions and answers. The judge made a note of this behaviour, but West told Johnny later that his interference should have been left unsaid.

Before the case came to court, Michael West had advised Johnny to ask his solicitor to draw up a list of people who could and would appear as witnesses to help Johnny's case. Johnny gave the matter some thought and decided – in spite of Marion's earlier advice that as he had no knowledge of the law, he should let his legal team deal with everything – that there were at least some aspects of the case that he would be the best judge of and the choosing of people who knew him and how he ran his business was one of them.

First, though, he hired a professional photographer to take pictures of his stock of boards, some covered against the weather, and some photographs showing the Honey board label. The police, of course, showed their own pictures of the similar boards they asserted had been dishonestly handled by Johnny and the two brothers.

As his first witness, Johnny had chosen his bank manager, Maurice Gardiner, who had known him since he opened his first bank account at the age of seventeen.

'When I went to him and told him I had been arrested,' Johnny said, 'his immediate reply was not to worry, and that it would soon be sorted out. So I knew he'd be a useful character witness. Besides, he was jovial, shrewd and full of wit.'

Maurice didn't exactly resemble everybody's idea of a bank manager; when he entered the box and took the oath, instead of the pin-striped dark suit, he was wearing a country-style tweed jacket and trousers and carrying a pork-pie hat. As Johnny's bank manager over the years, he had advised and helped him in every way he could. He was interested in this young man and his career and was proud he had helped to get him started. It was his theory that the job of a bank manager was to lend money in the belief that it would be returned in full, sometimes with an increase. He had not been disappointed in John Inkster.

Michael West was a skilled and experienced barrister and had, therefore, met every type of person, but was surprised that Maurice Gardiner would appear in a witness box. On a prompt from West, Maurice gave his name and address and said that he was manager of a branch of Barclays Bank.

'How long have you known Mr Inkster?' West asked.

'About ten or more years.'

'Would you say he was an honest man?'

'Oh, yes.'

The judge and prosecution had heard things like this before and their attention faded. Maurice, however, had come to show what kind of a young man Johnny was, so he continued: 'When John Inkster had a deal, he would often share it with the bank. Once he brought a lorry load of brand new dustbins that were cheap and good. He brought them right into the Gants Hill Branch of the bank and proceeded to sell them to the staff...' At this the judge woke up. The jury leaned forward. The prosecution paid attention. Maurice continued about how good these dustbins were and how much profit Johnny would make out of selling them. He knew how much they had cost him, because he had cashed a cheque the day before for the purchase. 'He was selling them at three times what they cost.'

By this time, Johnny realised Maurice Gardiner had the court in the palm of his hand. The judge and jury were sorry to see him go. There were no further questions.

The next witness Johnny had chosen had been the best man at his wedding. He was Wing Commander Gordon Hughes, a war hero pilot who had been instrumental in the sinking of the German battleship, *Tirpitz.*

Gordon Hughes gave similar evidence concerning Johnny's honest trading, adding: 'It was great being with him, watching him buying and selling bargains.' He had come all the way from Devon where he had become a farmer. 'Now, I think,' he complained, 'that the amount of expenses I am allowed to charge for my trip here is a pretty poor show.'

The judge interrupted him to say that he had authorised a larger amount of expenses in his case.

There was another immediate showing of 'thumbs up' from the little man at the front of the jury.

Another witness was to have been Johnny's old friend, Peter Hyland. Being an enthusiast of old cars, he arrived in St James's Square in a dilapidated and dirty 1930s Rolls Royce It was carrying on its roof a plywood collection. Peter was wearing a brown bowler hat. Michael West, seeing this eccentric arrival, obviously thought Peter wouldn't be a good proposition for the defence. Johnny, ruminating, said: 'I think West was afraid any evidence Peter gave might become funny and even farcical and get out of hand. West wanted to control every word spoken in the court. So Peter was dismissed without appearing.'

Then a woman called Vi Fairman, Johnny's part-time secretary, timidly took the stand as another character witness. Johnny had chosen her because she had always been protective of his reputation. If anyone even mildly criticised him – whoever they were – she would attack them. When she appeared in court she was highly nervous; she had never been in such a situation before. She had been well briefed by the solicitor, Alan Moore, as to what it would be like in the court, but as soon as she was cross-examined by the prosecution, she took offence at the allegations. They were attacking Johnny, so she shouted her protective protests. The two prosecution lawyers pressed and harried her and the more they did, the worse the atmosphere became. They took it in turns and tried every trick in their trade to attack Johnny in order to upset her into accidentally giving something away. The poor woman continued as best she could. Eventually the judge came to her rescue by saying: 'I think we've got the gist of this witness's evidence.'

Next came Geoffrey Silverman, the Jewish trader from whom Johnny had bought the fire-damaged boards. Placing a handkerchief on his head, he was sworn in on the Old Testament before being cross-examined.

'How much did you pay for these damaged boards?' West asked him. The cunning West was questioning this witness on the burnt boards in the hope the replies would highlight the fact that cheap boards were available and to dispel any accusation that Johnny should have known the Honey boards were sold too cheaply to be acquired honestly. However, West's ruse was not going to be achieved easily.

Mr Silverman declined to say.

West repeated his question. 'The damaged boards – how much did they cost you?'

'That's my private business,' Silverman insisted.

At this the judge took over. 'I'm afraid I must order you to tell us, Mr. Silverman.'

Silverman then produced a notebook, looked up his notes and said: 'I – um – paid sixpence each for them at the time.'

'I see.' said West, 'and for how much did you sell them for to my client, Mr Inkster?'

'Eight shillings.'

At this the judge leaned forward and said: 'It seems to me, Mr West, that you and I are in the wrong business.'

Laughter in court – and more thumbs up from the juryman.

The barrister representing the two farmer brothers was content to be led by West, because clearly it would follow that if Johnny was found to be not guilty, the brothers must also be. At this stage, West submitted that there was no case to answer. The judge, however, deemed that there was one.

But towards the end of that day's hearing, the judge stopped the case and addressed the jury. He told them that if they thought that anyone in the dock had no case to answer... 'You may go to the back of the court and you may arrive at a verdict of Not Guilty. You cannot, at this stage, find anyone guilty.' The jury indicated they would like to do this. Everyone waited in court and in about five minutes it was announced the jury had made a decision. When the jurors all returned, there were thumbs up again from the juryman and Johnny was again frightened of an accusation of collusion with him.

The jury's decision was that John Inkster and the two brothers were not guilty.

West, the great actor, relishing his success applied to the judge for costs.

My lord,' said West, bringing himself up to full height. 'Number one costs?

The judge's reply was short and sharp. 'No.'

'Ah… Number two, then?

'No,'

'Number three?'

A pause from the judge. 'Well – yes. Number Three.'

A nod and a smile from Michael West: 'As your Lordship pleases…'

Johnny heard later from a friend who knew about such things that it had paid to start high and drop down a category one by one as West had; you get a better deal than just asking for costs and letting the judge decide the amount.

Johnny's solicitor, Alan Moore, was paid four hundred pounds for his time and trouble. Michael West received his fee of eight hundred pounds, plus seventy-five for the initial briefing, plus the hundred pounds in cash for the case being thrown out of court.

Chapter Nine
A Man of Property

When Johnny's searches for further fortunes took him away from the wood markets, he rarely had much success. His various flutters into dog-breeding, pullet-dealing, meat-buying and dancing piglets were never entire failures, but the cash they put in his bank account was miniscule compared with the revenue acquired by dealing in sawdust and rejected timber of differing sorts from various places in the world.

To dabble, even mildly, in property had never crossed his mind; in any case the years he was building his fortune were not yet the ideal time to invest in bricks and mortar, and acreage to him only brought to mind somewhere he could keep a calf or a pig or two. So it was completely by chance that he even considered property for profit.

It all began at the south coast marina where he kept his boat, the thirty-two foot Grand Banks. Having won the Old Bailey court case and collected his costs, he decided to celebrate by investing in a larger boat for the family. A thirty-six foot Grand Banks would cost sixteen thousand pounds, so he would have to sell the old one to top up the money. While he was thinking about it, Marion told her father that Johnny was buying a new boat. Immediately Percy telephoned.

Johnny told him that he had hoped to part-exchange the old one for the new, but it turned out that wouldn't work. 'How much do you want for the old one?' his father-in-law asked.

'Ten grand.'

'But you only paid nine thousand, two fifty for it two years ago.'

'Ah yes,' Johnny explained, 'but today it would cost twelve thousand.'

Johnny remembered the scene well. 'Those were the wonderful days of great inflation. So, after a bit more argy-bargy Perce agreed to pay ten grand, but warned me not to tell Joan – she didn't like it at the Hamble marina, or the Solent waters. Prefers the Thames for boating. Anyhow, I told him that I wanted his cheque by Friday. I didn't want Mum-in-law putting a block on both deals I had made.'

Slightly indignant, Percy told him: 'I have always paid on the dot immediately. I have never had any bank loans, or extended credit. Not even hire purchase.' He was a proud man. 'Come to my factory today and I will give you the cheque.'

'What about Mum-in-law?'

'Leave that to me.'

Johnny collected his cheque and later that afternoon Marion received a call from her father. 'When you phone Mum tonight, he suggested slyly, 'just tell her that I have bought your boat.'

Marion loved her father dearly but could see through his ruse and thought it better to stand well back, so suggested gently it would be better for him to break the news himself.

Percy ran the boat in the south coast marina for about a year, then sold it for a three thousand pound profit and returned to boating on the Thames.

Johnny and his family became acquainted with the many types of people who came in and out of that marina near Southampton. He often nodded a 'good morning' to the prime minister of the day, Edward Heath, as he took

145

Sunday off from the problems of Downing Street to sail down the Solent. There were business tycoons of all sorts and men from nearby villages out for a day's fishing. It didn't matter that they were all different types, or ages, even some different nationalities, they all had a common interest – the boat, whether a large or small one that would, they each hoped, get them safely from A to B and back again.

Johnny's interest in the Grand Banks type of boat brought him other contacts. 'I was once moored alongside a man who owned a fifty-foot Grand Banks – a sizeable ship. Of course we got talking. He was a builder and property developer and had a string of holiday camps all along the south coast. His name was Bert Figgins.

'It wasn't long before I'd sold him a load of plywood, chipboard and timber. He sometimes drove over to Essex to buy various stuff from me.

'We talked a lot. He was a great entrepreneur; made his money buying up old Army camps and converting them into holiday camps in the early 50s. He was also in the demolition business, knocking down parts of stately homes and such like, because during the Attlee Government they had put such heavy taxes on big country houses that the owners had either to demolish parts of their houses or open them to the public for a fee to enable the tax to be paid.

'He had also built a house for himself in the middle of a woodland not far from our marina.'

Johnny's friendship with Bert Figgins lasted on good social and business terms until one day he heard that Bert – a big, fat man in his sixties, but still very energetic, had collapsed and died from a heart attack, leaving his family with heavy death duties and taxes on his various properties. His wife and daughter were left with little but bills.

146

About a year later, Johnny had a phone call from the distressed daughter asking if he would come to the house in the woods, which was also Bert's builders' yard, and possibly be interested in buying back some of the plywood and timber that he had sold her father. It didn't sound to Johnny like a very profitable journey, to drive over just to buy back a couple of lorry loads of timber, so he put it off for a while. A second call from the daughter pricked his conscience and he and Marion drove to the house.

Bert's daughter met them, showed them round the yard and Johnny ended up buying most of the various machines, building materials, and scaffolding, in fact everything there was to run a builder's yard.

In passing, Johnny had a good look at the house – a fine building. 'What's happening to the house' he asked casually.

'It's up for sale.'

'How much do you want for it?'

'Make me an offer.'

'Forty thousand pounds,'

'It's not much but I'll put it to the bank. When can you pay and complete?'

'Seven days.'

She telephoned the bank then and there. Putting down the phone, she said: 'You now own this house.'

So this was Johnny Inkster's abrupt entry into the property market – about which he knew little or nothing.

He and Marion drove home and as soon as they arrived, he looked up his accounts. He had, it appeared, forty thousand pounds in his bank account, which was his company's money. There were also a few bits and pieces in private accounts.

He telephoned his accountant and told him: 'I have just bought a house, a builder's yard and seven acres of woods and landscaped gardens in the south of England. All for forty thousand.'

The accountant, a friendly fellow, but still an accountant asked: 'Where's the money? Do you want me to arrange a mortgage?'

'No; not necessary. I've got the forty grand in my bank.'

'You may well have,' the accountant replied, 'but I am working on an Inland Revenue inquiry into you, and if it goes wrong you will end up paying thirty thousand pounds to them.'

Johnny's next move was to go from his house to Percy's nearby residence where he announced: 'Marion and I have just bought a house in a wood and a posh garden for forty grand near the south coast.'

'Then you must be mad,' was Percy's reply. 'For that money you could buy the whole of a county on the south coast, the way the property market is at the moment.'

This was pretty deflating news for a man who was used to making a profit from every transaction, even when it was a tiny one. His recent hope of suggesting that Percy come in with him on the deal was postponed for the moment. Instead, he suggested that Percy came down to the property with him the next day and look over the building machinery and other items he had also purchased. Percy could help him transport some of it back to Essex and maybe would be interested in buying one or two things for himself from Johnny's purchases.

'Of course I'll come to help carry it back,' said Percy with a sly smile, 'but if there's nothing there that I want, I'll charge you forty quid for the day's haulage.'

Next day the two men set off going south west from Essex. As he drove up the drive to the house, an elegant mansion, Percy was clearly impressed and as the car came to rest in the driveway he said: 'So, do you want me to come half way with you on the house?'

Knowing that he had no idea what to do with the house he had bought, and having learnt also that there might be an expensive tax problem, Johnny decided it would be insane not to do a fifty-fifty deal with Percy. As he nodded his agreement, Percy handed over a cheque for twenty thousand pounds. When he arrived home, Johnny immediately sent off his cheque for the whole amount and they now owned house and grounds with all fixtures, fittings and some furniture.

As the new joint-owner, Percy's first question was what they were going to do with the property. And Johnny had his answer ready.

'We are going to sell timber and chipboard and such like from the builders' yard. One day, when the property market improves – if ever – we could think of selling the lot for a nice profit.'

Johnny knew that Bert Figgins had originally acquired about twenty-five acres attached to the property and had been approached by a co-operative society in search of land in the area to build a massive hypermarket. They had purchased an option from Figgins and if planning permission was granted they would buy and build. Within about three years, they did just that.

In the meantime, Percy and Johnny bided their time and set up a thriving wood sale business, because their type of building material was hard to buy then. For several years their successful business attracted hundreds of eager local clients.

Every Saturday morning the two men drove to the yard to work there, stacking and sorting and selling timber. On their way from Essex they would take the A3 in Surrey and stop for their breakfast at a Little Chef roadside diner to relax and read the daily papers supplied for customers. On the homeward run, they would make a dangerous U-turn across the lane of traffic racing the other way to stop at the same place for the tea and toast Percy demanded. Several times Johnny suggested they drive on a little further and take their tea at Hindhead's Happy Eater which was on their side of the road.

'Too expensive,' Percy decreed, so Johnny still had to make the dangerous double crossing for their cuppa.

After some years of successful trading at their new yard, they received the letter Johnny had always been hoping for. It was from a London estate agent who wrote asking if they owned the seven acre estate and house, as he had a customer who would like to discuss the purchase. The client, interested in property development, would like to meet the owners as soon as possible.

Obviously Johnny and Percy agreed to meet the client on the site.

Over their Little Chef breakfast the next Saturday morning, Johnny and Percy discussed the prospective offer.

'No selling out for nothing,' announced Percy.

'No fear.' Johnny agreed.

'What sort of figure do you have in mind, Johnny?'

'One million.' It was not a question, it was an announcement.

'Exactly. You've hit the nail on the head.'

As they mulled over the details in their minds they drove on to the site, to be there when the development agent arrived.

His shiny car drew up at the appointed time and a man in a shiny suit got out, announcing an immediate implication that his company was one of the biggest in the universe and having already studied an Ordnance Survey map of the area, he would like to make an immediate offer.

Percy butted in without ceremony with: 'We are not poor people anxious to sell, and we are looking for something substantial.'

'I would like to offer three million,' the man replied.

Johnny hastily disguised a surprised and sudden missing heartbeat and noted Percy had turned a little grey about the gills.

The would-be purchaser outlined his firm's offer for an option to purchase lasting two years subject to planning permission. If planning permission was granted, well and good for the three million purchase price. If it wasn't granted, there would be no deal.

It all sounded all right, but was not something they completely understood. However, it seemed they were not poor any more, so when the man had gone they decided to shut up shop for the night and go home to tell Marion and Joan their news.

When they reached the Little Chef area on the A3, Johnny began to manoeuvre his U-turn, Percy stopped him saying: 'I think we can afford to continue to the Happy Eater at Hindhead today.'

Johnny's part-time secretary, Vi, was very proud of her son, Eddy, who had a degree from the London School of Economics and now had a job with a property developer. Johnny thought it might be an idea to run the details of his current deal and option past the young man and see what he had to say. He began telling the story, but before he got very far, Vi's son interrupted him saying: 'Don't sign anything. I will give you ten thousand for the same option plus three and a half million and ten percent of our profits should planning permission be granted. I'll come down and have a look at the place tomorrow.'

So the two eager sellers drove south again next day. Johnny asked Eddy what the London agent's idea was. Seeing the Co-op's supermarket already near the woodland site, he suggested they might be the interested party.

'If it is to offer it to the Co-op people,' Johnny pondered, 'why wouldn't they – if they were interested in expansion – come direct to me?'

Eddy shook his head. 'Not when they hear that I am going to sell to Sainsbury's…'

'How do you know Sainsbury's would be interested in this site?'

'When I tell them it is next door to a Co-op, they'll want it.'

'How about planning permission?'

'No problem. Every council wants a Sainsbury's.'

He duly paid the ten thousand and the option for two years was signed.

Even two years later, after negotiations with the Co-op and the local authority, Eddy's company never did apply for planning permission.

The two Essex men tallied their score like a football match.

Percy and Johnny: ten thousand. Others: nil.

Not long afterwards, the Co-op telephoned. 'Your option has run out,' they announced.

'Yes,' Johnny replied, 'we know. And I expect the Co-op will be pleased.'

'Well,' came the reply. 'Will you sell us an option instead?'

'Yes, for ten thousand pounds.'

'Our solicitor will be in touch...'

The Co-op's option ran for two years, but they were unable to complete. The score now was Percy and Johnny: Twenty thousand. Others: Nil.

Eventually, the great Co-op hypermarket was sold to Asda. Then one day Johnny heard that Asda had bought a similar parcel of land north of their plot, so he picked up the telephone and made a call to their offices in Leeds.

'If you are buying land to expand, we can offer you some to the south of you.'

They sent an agent to look, and made an offer of four million to be exchanged at the end of the option providing the granting of planning permission.

Now having learnt about this option business, Johnny replied: 'An option for two years would be twenty thousand.'

They agreed and paid. But they never did apply for planning permission and Johnny never heard from them again.

Score: Percy and John: forty thousand pounds. Others: nil.

Meanwhile, there is a huge Asda Supermarket just beyond the end of their garden…

Because of their 'winnings' in the property market, and because their timber market in the south was still prospering, Percy and Johnny were always on the lookout for another possibility, especially now they had surplus cash to invest. When they heard that Hobbs Cross Farm at Epping was on the market they became interested. The farm sale included five hundred acres of arable land, five hundred milking cows, a small flock of sheep and fifty breeding sows, which had been farmed successfully by William Collins and his wife for several years. Johnny knew the history of Hobbs Cross Farm very well. In fact when it had been owned by the British Oil and Cattle Mill Company as a training ground for young farmers, his very first career move had been to apply for a job there. It had then been his ambition to become a farmer, and he had felt a job with BOCM would give him experience. But he'd been turned down.

As a demonstration farm originally, the cow sheds, pig sties and other buildings had been built with viewing galleries where visiting farmers or farm students had been able to watch the farming processes and animals at close quarters.

BOCM had similar farms all over the country, so decided to sell Hobbs Cross Farm and concentrate on their other venues. Collins bought it in the early nineteen sixties, originally farming in a normal manner, until he discovered that one or two local schools had contacted his farm manager to ask if they could bring some of their pupils who were learning about the production of food. The manager had agreed. Within a few weeks, Collins noticed that several school parties with about fifty or sixty children each had visited and his farm staff of tractor drivers, management, and farm workers were spending more time on the school visits than working on the farm.

As Collins was an enterprising young man, full of energy and also in need of further financial support, it occurred to him that if he sent a mail-shot to all the schools in the area, and turned a couple of unused barns into school-rooms fitted out with school desks and notice boards containing farming information, he could charge one pound per child per visit. He also thought of employing one or two of the mothers as guides, to come along after taking their own children to school. He arranged coaches to pick up the children from the schools, bring them to the farm around ten thirty in the morning, and take them back to their schools at two-thirty, which would give the mother-guides time to pick up their own children from their schools...

It developed into a great business. In a short while the farm had some two or three hundred children visiting each day and gradually extended to about the same number of other visitors. Collins mailed schools all over East London as well and turned a field into a car park to hold more than two hundred cars and several London buses.

Kids who had visited a couple of times so enjoyed the experience that on returning home they would entice their parents and brothers and sisters to visit Hobbs Cross Farm at weekends. Collins then converted a piggery into a café selling sandwiches and snacks, and later a calf-shed into male and female toilets; he turned another shed into a farm and gift shop and added a large activity playground.

The enterprise prospered for fourteen to fifteen years. Then came the sale of the farm. Some local farmers bought plots of the farmland which bordered their own properties, but the majority of the buildings with their excellent observation galleries and about forty acres were put up separately for sale.

Johnny and his father-in-law decided to buy it and to develop their timber business into a leisure venture.

Johnny, always a farmer at heart, loved owning the cattle, pigs, sheep – and added poultry. When his animals went to slaughter, their meat was sold to an eager public in the farm shop. They decided to enlarge the café and turn it into a restaurant with seating for a hundred and twenty people; the decor and menu were based on the farm scene. The numbers of children arriving each day gradually increased to some five hundred in spring and summer. When winter came, Johnny's son Mark had the idea of forming a Comedy Club where young comedians would come and entertain, performing to a local audience on a small stage erected in the restaurant. The charge per head for the evening was ten pounds, which included a basket containing Hobbs Cross spare-ribs and chips. Marion applied for and was granted a licence to sell alcohol. The whole family, including Percy and Joan, worked eighteen hours a day for seven days a week.

Their leisure enterprise was extremely successful and cost effective – but jolly hard work. After about eight years Percy, now in his eighties, became ill and could no longer work at Hobbs Cross Farm. Joan also had to retire because her long days now had to be spent looking after her ailing husband.

'It had been entirely a family-fun business,' Johnny sighed in regret. 'But, with two of the helpful hands no longer able to help, and the rest of us over-working to take up their loss it began to be clear that one day we would have to give up Hobbs Cross Farm. It would be a bonanza for anyone who wanted to buy a successful business, plus a farm and land.

Chapter 10
The Property Researcher

During the momentary lull that came into Johnny's life and career after the closure of Hobb's Cross Farm, he stopped for a while one day to wonder what it was that had brought him his successes so far, and to assess whether it could be repeated.

It was not, he confessed to himself, as if he knew anything, or was trained to do anything. His mind wandered back to the very beginnings of his business life. It wasn't all that easy at first, but he'd enjoyed it. For example, the Jewish furniture manufacturers whose surplus sawdust he obtained free in order to sell to the farmers were probably the best joke-tellers in the country and he listened carefully then repeated them to the East Anglian farmers who, by and large in those days seemed to him a pretty miserable, tight-fisted lot. But his business was based on humour; he had nothing else.

'Yes,' he said; 'That was it. The sawdust business to me was all based on humour, fun and wit. I was sorry when it ended. But in monetary terms chipboard and plywood had overtaken sawdust. I was by then using the property I'd bought in the south as a market place to sell the rejects I was still obtaining from overseas. It's still doing well. Then Hobbs Cross made a third business. But now that's gone.'

What's next?

In the curious coincidental way that things happened to Johnny, he heard a rumour in Five Oaks Lane where he and Percy lived that, despite the worst depression in the property market since the turn of the century, a property researcher was trying to buy the Lane's thirty-four or so houses, each of which had between a quarter of an acre and four acres of land attached. It seemed the idea was to develop it all into new houses. Of course it was an attractive site for an ambitious developer, but it was an impossible developer's dream because the lane was in the Metropolitan green belt where no building was allowed.

Within a day or two of hearing the rumour, a letter arrived for Johnny. The letter-heading announced it was from Alexander Research, and Johnny noticed that there were no names listed on the billhead but a posh address and office in the new London Docklands. The letter was signed by a Mr Tony Hunt, who explained that he represented a company of property developers and was investigating whether planning permission could be granted for an estate of houses, if his company purchased the whole of Five Oaks Lane.

Working on his recent experience in Hampshire where developers tried to buy options, Johnny thought it wouldn't be too difficult to out-face this Mr Hunt, and might be a bit of fun. So he wrote back with what he thought was a pretty smart and witty letter.

'Send a cheque,' Johnny wrote, 'and, if sufficient, we will send our deeds by return. If not sufficient, we won't bother to cash your cheque.'

'All very clever,' he later confessed. 'But I hadn't met Tony Hunt then.'

In fact, it turned out that Tony Hunt had been a very skilled negotiator for the purchase of land over the years for several major house-building companies in the City and was now trying his hand on his own. He needed one big deal which could make millions overnight. And maybe this was it.

His current idea was to knock on the door of every house in the lane, having written previously outlining his 'research' company's idea. On meeting an owner, Hunt would ask if he would consider selling. He expected at this stage that the answer was likely to be 'No'. So then he would explain that he would buy the property for three times its current value. It wasn't going to be an easy transaction. It was likely that the owner of such a house in such a place already had a small business which he could adequately run from his home. He was not likely to be short of money, and was quite happy to live out the rest of his days right where he was, in Five Oaks Lane.

After all, it was a pretty useful area to live in. The properties backed on to two major golf courses; were just over a mile from Central Line tube and there were buses available to run into the nearest major town of Romford. These were all good reasons for the lane's house owners to stay put and also good reasons for property developers to want the land to build more and better housing there.

Naturally Tony, the wily researcher, had several strategies up his sleeve. He would explain to the potential seller that he had already seen a number of the Five Oaks Lane neighbours, and some were considering selling. He would then politely make his exit, suggesting he would leave them to think about the idea, and would come back in about a week.

He knew the power of the dream he was leaving them with. While most of the owners were happy to stay where they were, had no mortgages nor bank loans, nor any real money troubles – there was something about the huge offer of three times the value that could disturb sleep at nights and even bring daytime dreams, in addition to the possibility of buying a smaller, easier to run, more modern house… and probably enough cash over to buy another for a grown up son or daughter, or maybe a family holiday flat or villa in Spain… and enough change to salt away on deposit for some rainy day. The difference that amount of money could make to their lives would be a great temptation.

Within a week or two Tony Hunt had signed options to buy, subject to planning permission, several of the lane's properties. His snowball had been made and was now rolling downhill and getting bigger as it went.

So now he had to tackle the green belt problem. He had already been to meet the planning officers of the local authority and had been told, in no uncertain terms that green belt meant no building. However, it seemed as though the council hated Five Oaks Lane and most of the people who lived and worked there. They possibly considered it scruffy and run down with property filled with various businesses that had developed and grown since the war and had flourished without any planning permission or authority.

Johnny believed that later, at another meeting, the would-be developer had cleverly pointed out to the planning officers that if he purchased the whole lane, and cleared out all the houses and businesses, he was sure he could return twenty-five percent of the unauthorised land to the green belt, and he would build on the seventy-five percent of what was already there. Johnny reckoned that the council had most likely replied that he would have to buy the whole of the lane – and this would be talking in terms of many millions. But, if he could do that, they would agree to support an application. So, now, Tony would be armed with a letter to this effect from the local architect. He could now talk to banks, financiers, builders and so on – all the people whose help he would need to achieve his ambitious dreams. Tony would be in clover, Johnny decided.

Tony Hunt's next move was to seek out the owners of the two biggest properties in Five Oaks Lane. So John Inkster at The Chippings received a phone call: 'Could we meet?'

Johnny was amazed when he met this slick operator. 'He had already researched me and the whole of my family. He knew everything – how I lived; how many children I had; who my in-laws were; my hobbies – everything. He even knew that on his first visit he would have to sit at the breakfast bar.' He had heard that in Johnny and Marion's house, all business was conducted in the kitchen. It also came as no surprise to Mr Hunt that Marion's father, who owned the largest plot of land in the area, was ill but would be represented by his daughter Marion. Tony Hunt knew well that the Inksters and the Beaumonts lived in the centre of the lane and therefore Marion was very important in representing both properties.

Johnny began his usual sales pitch, cups of coffee, jokes, and stories, but quickly realised he was up against a very smart operator. 'Much cleverer than I will ever be,' Johnny admitted. 'But I did have my earlier experience of options to fall back on and insisted on a two-year option, subject to planning permission, and for this I would want twenty thousand pounds, and Marion would want the same for her father.'

When Johnny put that offer to him, Tony departed to advise his associates who were now becoming interested in the venture. Within a week there was more coffee, a few more amusing jokes around Johnny's breakfast bar and two cheques for the required amounts were forthcoming, And, so the deal was done. The price offered was three times what the properties were worth with an option to buy within three years if planning was granted.

The council granted planning permission for as many applications as had arrived from Five Oaks Lane but things were not yet all plain sailing for Tony. While waiting for the permission to materialise, he had approached a builder whose firm was big enough to tackle the mass of demolition and rebuilding that would be required. When the planning came through, apparently Tony saw the builder with a view to asking him to buy some of the properties. But the builder turned him down. It seemed he wanted to buy up the whole of the properties in the Lane with planning permission by way of an option. After much argument, there was no agreement and Johnny believed the builder had suggested Tony advertise for another builder, knowing that he was virtually working within a closed shop. Tony approached other big builders, but the answer was always, 'No, you already have a good builder.'

At the time he had bought the options to Five Oaks Lane he had registered the properties with the Land Registry, so by the time the options expired – with or without planning permission – Tony Hunt would still have a lien to purchase.

In the meantime, Johnny was busy thinking about his own position and how to protect it. Supposing Tony failed to take up his options – now nearing their end – and another developer decided to build new houses for sale? Johnny's cunning preventative measure to this possible deal was to apply to the council for a change of use on his property. He requested that his business be changed from handling woodchips and sawdust, to the building of an abattoir and for the rendering of bones and animal fats. He knew very well that a change of use to this unattractive business with associated unpleasant fragrances would have to be advertised and that any local property owners or prospective purchasers could voice objections. Especially as at that time the whole of Britain was pre-occupied with the BSE cattle disease sweeping the

162

country. Things could be infinitely delayed to Johnny's tune.

As soon as Johnny's two year option expired and the planning permission had also been granted, Tony Hunt had to tell Johnny that he intended to take up the option to buy and pay up within twenty-eight days. If the money was not forthcoming by that time, the option would end and Johnny would hold the contract. Tony was therefore in a position where he had to find the money to buy, not only Johnny's and Percy's, but all the houses in Five Oaks Lane. It seems he had reason to believe that help would come from the builder, who on the day of completion of all the properties in the Lane, could buy them from Tony as one whole parcel. The builder, however, decided that he was not going to do that; he was not buying the properties from Tony.

Tony tried desperately for what was left of the month to find another builder, but failed.

Johnny and Percy, now the option period had come to an end, were in a position to find another buyer. Johnny approached the builder, who wanted the property, but offered a smaller amount than Hunt had originally offered. In any case, nothing could be done as Tony Hunt still had a lien on the properties in the Lane.

It began to look like a gridlock.

Eventually, however, the builder contacted Johnny to ask if he could get the lien lifted, adding that if Johnny was successful he would renew Hunt's original offer and pay three times what the property was worth.

As it appeared that nothing would happen, nothing would be forthcoming to bring matters to a conclusion unless he lent a hand, Johnny took up the challenge... He telephoned Tony's London solicitors asking them to get the lien lifted on his property. But there was only a silence from the solicitor, so he telephoned again and again several times a day, eventually even threatening to report them to the Law Society. 'You are supposed to deal with this matter at arm's length, now the option has expired,' he told them. The repeated threats eventually worked, the solicitor gave up and Tony's lien was lifted.

So Johnny was able to deal direct with the builder who by now was buying up all the Five Oaks properties that Tony Hunt had been forced to abandon. Everything went satisfactorily; the builder agreed to the price at three times what the property was worth and told Johnny that the legal side of his work was in the hands of his London solicitor.

Johnny and Marion thought it would speed things up if they went to London themselves to collect the builder's two money drafts – one for their own property and the other for Percy's – from the solicitor. They both thought this would be a good and secure idea, because they could just pick up the drafts and take them straight to the London branch of their local bank. Unfortunately their appointment with the solicitor was cancelled for a worrying three days, before they could take the trip and collect the cash.

As they were finally leaving the solicitor's to go to their London bank, Johnny told the solicitor: 'We shall be going straight home – I suppose the house will still be ours for tonight?'

And so it was time for the family to move. Johnny, Marion and Mark bade farewell to their native Essex and decided to live in the Hampshire house they had owned now for some years but never used as a home.

'No regrets,' said Johnny, 'I had often thought that part of the country would be better for my type of business – and have, in fact, been running it there very successfully for some time.' Jennie, who was now married and with a young family of her own, soon followed with her husband, to a place nearby.

Since then, some might have thought that Johnny would retire, but not so, retirement from work was not in his nature. Instead, he has enlarged the trading side to include the sale of do-it-yourself kits for building log cabins – some large enough for houses with several rooms; some small enough for garden sheds or offices. And, of course, this still keeps Johnny in the wood business in a different way.

He and Marion nowadays have good holidays on board a newer, bigger boat moored in an elegant marina in Antibes. While they sun themselves in France, the business is cared for by Mark, himself a trader by nature and with a college business degree, and also by son-in-law, Robert.

No amount of work or restful holidays deter Johnny's mind from spotting problems to solve, or from seeking out answers that have stirred his mind even to questions of national importance… Sometimes it is the local or national press which receives his questions. More often his local member of parliament or some other politician he feels might explain. His most recent personal campaign has been to try to fathom the real reasons for local governments' keen desire to collect waste paper, cardboard, tins, some plastic, all for recycling. Why do they want the stuff? Where do they put it all? Who does what with it and where is the sorting done?

But, even if he gets satisfactory answers to all his questions, that won't be the end of his quests – some other will come into view and his mind will be off again, seeking explanations, answers, excuses.

Ever since his days discovering the Terenure Club, Johnny has been a party lover – and what better occasion to celebrate with a party than the Ruby Wedding of the happy marriage of Johnny and Marion? And so it was organised.

The venue was the Royal Southern Yacht Club (whose blue ensign always decorates the yacht in Antibes) in the Hampshire village of Hamble. The several hundred guests were members of family, friends and associates they had met and known over the years. There were farmers and wood merchants, solicitors and accountants, boating mates – wives and husbands and some children. The men were splendid in their dinner jackets and black ties; the feminine guests added colour, elegance and sparkle to the occasion in their ball gowns and jewellery. Even the children showed off their party gear.

There was an extravagant buffet where guests could help themselves to a fantastic banquet. There was wine on every table and a bar in the room if you fancied a different drink.

The wedding reception of Johnny and Marion at the Red House pub had been as sweet and simple and sincere as were the dreams and aspirations then of the young couple themselves... The Ruby celebration forty years later retained a touch of the simplicity, much of the sincerity, with the addition of the glamour that the realisation of those hopes and ambitions had brought to them.

As they laughed and joked and talked and reminisced with their many friends in the Yacht Club's ballroom upstairs, the lonely figure of another boating member ate alone at a table for one – it was the ex-Prime Minister of England, Sir Edward Heath, Johnny's neighbour in the marina, who had been invited to join the party but had excused himself on the grounds of exhaustion after a hard day's sailing.

Heath was a carpenter's son from Kent, across the Thames from Johnny's Essex. He had presumably grown up in a world of sawdust, off-cuts of wood, and chippings. But he clearly never realised they could have a financial value and he missed an opportunity.

LaVergne, TN USA
12 August 2010
193089LV00002B/18/P